nakedLEADERSHIP
Leading From The Inside Out

Mark W. Gregory Ph.D.

nakedLEADERSHIP
- Leading From The Inside Out -

Published by Mark W. Gregory
N L Project - Murfreesboro, TN

Scriptural translations and paraphrases: Mark W Gregory
Cover Design and Interior Layout: Mark W. Gregory

And I will give them shepherds who have my own heart;
they will provide them knowledge and wisdom.

Jeremiah 3:15

nakedLeadership

Foreword

Having studied, taught and modeled leadership for over twenty years, I've come to the conclusion that being a leader is a journey of ups and downs, spits and spurts, and moments of brilliance followed by episodes of foolhardiness. These occurrences often leave me with an abrupt, "oops, why did I do that?" Sometimes I feel as though "I don't know anything about leadership," but that very admission is a step forward as a leader. It creates a thirst to reflect on my journey, understand what I've experienced, and extrapolate lessons for the future. I've learned a lot, and I know there's a lot more to learn.

So, at this point in my leadership journey I can rightly ask: what do I now know about leadership after serving in the trenches with many perplexing, complex, and gut wrenching decisions? In the following pages I'll answer this question, but in doing so, I will probably reveal more of *who I am* than *what you should do.* Truly a priority, the first task of the leader is to answer the question: Who Am I?

But certainly there are principles or tested practices - I prefer to call them disciplines - that have guided me through some tortuous times. At the very least these disciplines have improved my understanding of how I function in leadership. They include: determining personal identity, defining leadership, developing transparency, understanding my default style, and forfeiting leadership. Some of these themes are worthy of chapters, others are thoughts that will be threaded throughout a number of the chapters. All are serious, root issues for any leader.

The title "nakedLEADERSHIP" captures some of the difficulty faced by leaders. We are exposed and vulnerable, constantly under the crucible of scrutiny by our peers and critics. That's the external perspective. Yet, the greatest component of naked leadership is the question of who we are internally and how this affects our interaction with others. When you strip everything away from our lives, or take it all off to reveal the core of who we are, what's really left? Do we have a strong enough sense of our personhood? Do we have the personal reserves and resources to remain intact emotionally and spiritually? That is when the true core of a leader is disclosed!

We, as leaders, face great horizons in leading our organizations forward and we often face significant opposition and setbacks that wound us professionally. Let's also admit these challenge sometimes cripple us emotionally. The successful leaders somehow press on, discover new opportunities, envision more options, cast new vision, and generally persevere to the end. They are the ones who keep standing when others have fallen away. They arrive at port when many desert the floundering ship. The resurrection, rebirth, or renewal of a static organization is a painful process, one not entered lightly or grasped too quickly without reflection. Nonetheless, the one who stands at the helm at the end of the journey is commonly declared the leader.

So, here we go! Learn from my pilgrimage, if you will, but learn from your own even more. Maybe the co-incidence of my journey will somehow help you on yours.

I'll see you standing at the end, at the helm, and we'll declare you the leader!

SECTION ONE

___

Beginning with Self

The reality is that leadership is more about
"who we are" than "what we do,"
and that truth sheds light on how we gauge success.

CHAPTER 1

Root: Who am I?

"I am root" is a tee shirt slogan humorously implying that everything revolves around self, specifically the wearer of the shirt. The idea developed from the software world where root is the originating directory from which a file is launched. As such, it is the essential location of the executable process, and from there a code loads into the computer's memory and "runs." Every program operates from the directions found in the root directory.

Root also refers to the base or origin of a word in its earliest historical meaning or the most reducible form. For instance, the root of the noun "application" is the verb "apply." Actually, most words have a lineage that can be traced through various languages to an originating concept. So, as a term of our day, root is focused on determining the source, the origin, or the core of something.

For the leader, to consider root is to discover the remnant of his or her identity after peeling back the outer shell of self. In essence, what's at the core of who I am? I've often asked myself the question, "If I strip everything away, who am I?" This is not an easy determination, for it approaches the elusive "what's the meaning of life" question; yet, it is a means of examining our personal core and belief in who we are as individuals. The desire to understand more of who we are at our nucleus is a legitimate pursuit, though it may be painful at times. It forces us to determine the criteria of self worth and the values we assign them. Unfortunately, we often have depended on the wrong things to feel better about ourselves.

Are we *what we do*? Some affirm quickly that who we are is in reality a presentation of what we do. Thus, the accomplishments we accumulate become the defining sum-total of who we are. It becomes our self presentation. We base our value as persons and leaders on what we've done (past personal history) or how well we do our job (present performance evaluation). Our emotions rise with exuberance at a job well done and fall into despondency when we lose our jobs or our endeavors fail.

We're trained to think in this way; it's the default mode for us. For example, when you meet someone new, your initial questions might be reminiscent of the proverbial introduction as you're seated on a plane. "What's your name, and what do you do?" Ring a bell? "Who are you" is the real underlying question, but it's never worded that way – fundamentally because we, too, often incorrectly equate who we are with what we do.

I'm a good one to fall into this category. As a motivated, goal oriented person, it's easy for me to point to the professional and personal trappings of my life and say, "this is who I am." I'm the kind of guy who once he starts something is likely to finish it. For example, there are only a handful of books I've started to read that I never finished. I will gut it out even if I find the content boring or poorly written. There's something in me that prompts the "finish it" mentality. That positive character trait translates into almost every area of my life, and pushes me to start and hang with an endeavor persistently until the deed is accomplished.

One of my ventures, a karate black belt, actually was a carry over from my teenage years where I started but didn't finish my training. It was one of those things that I always said, "one day I want to finish it." Fast forward three decades to the age of thirty-nine – an unlikely age to begin martial arts training. Not only did I achieve a first degree black belt, but also a second degree, and an instructor's certificate, eventually leading the martial arts school through my church. In another pursuit, I began training and obtained a pilot's license at the age of forty-three and later completed my instrument rating at age of forty-eight. In my forties, I ran the half-marathon three times, and hope to do so again - perhaps in my fifties. This summary gives you some indication of my professional and personal pursuits. But do these things define me? No, they do not.

My friends know me well; they know my personality traits since they've observed my professional and personal journey. I'm not abrasive or abrupt in what I do, and not necessarily a Type-A personality. One friend described me to an acquaintance, "He's the most passive man I know." There are many who might disagree with that assertion, and personally, I hope it's not entirely true - I think what they were trying to say is that I'm easy to get along with or can roll with the punches. Regardless, I'm a highly relational person who enjoys friendships and activities with others. I'm also a determined person who simply starts and doesn't stop until a project is finished.

Not long ago I purchased a heavy duty spring-loaded stapler for attaching upholstery to a boat seat frame. After only a few shots it jammed and my initial attempts to clear it proved unsuccessful. It was broken and useless. I could have returned it, but decided to take it apart - only to have the case spring apart when I removed the screws. Despite appearances, it's not a simple mechanism and the parts could fit in numerous configurations. I worked on and off for three days, trying different combinations, visualizing the pieces and how they might reassemble. Finally, I flipped a small spring over in a different way, slipped the case together and ... it worked. It took persistence, patience, and a determination to not let the device beat me. Another accomplishment!

So, I have finished a lot of starts and persevered through many projects – and, oh, how easy it would be to take those accomplishments and say: "this is who I am." I'm a pastor, pilot, martial arts black belt, runner, or author. From a family perspective, I could say I'm a husband, father, or son.

Yet, we must concede that these answers fall short of really identifying the core person. The inherent danger is that if I identify myself by these things, what happens when they don't go well? If I claim to be a successful pastor when my church explodes in growth, then who am I if my church isn't doing well? Would I be as quick to say, I'm an "unsuccessful pastor." To paraphrase a friend of mine: If you take credit for the growth of your church, will you take credit for the demise of the same? Put the negative into each of these categories and reason it through: I'm an unsuccessful father, husband, runner, pastor, author - Ouch!

It's not that we settle for mediocrity and accept or prejudge ourselves to be unsuccessful, nor is it that we cast every measure of success to the wind. Rather we learn to gauge and understand the true scope of success. The reality is that leadership is more about "who we are" than "what we do," and that truth sheds light on how we gauge success.

> *The reality is that leadership is more about "who we are" than "what we do," and that truth sheds light on how we gauge success.*

If the first task of the leader is to ask, "who am I?," we need a different path of reasoning to determine that answer. There's really only one legitimate framework that will sustain us and allow us to persevere regardless of the circumstances. That model is our relationship with God through Christ - to know and be known by God, to be defined as someone of worth in Him. This is root: to be loved, accepted, and known as we are. If you take it all away, I still have root. I still have God. I still have Christ.

One of the greatest leaders of the Old Testament, King David, asked this question of the Lord, "who am I?" when he received the word from the prophet that the Lord would build a house for him, and his lineage would be upheld forever. (1 Chronicles 17:16). The answer was not in what David would do in his kingship, and we admit that David had a number of miserable failures. Ultimately God's favor in his life was based on the aspect of David's private and corporate worship and his intimate relationship with God. He was subsequently known as a man after God's own heart.

The relational perspective of our worth is noted in the Hebrew word for God - Yahweh. The root name is often rendered, "I AM." It is a difficult name to grasp fully since it can be translated in past, present, or future tenses, and even given a causative emphasis. But doesn't that sum it up? I AM! It is an affirmation of eternal existence and causative power in relationship with all creation, cosmos, and yes, even us as created beings. If the root of God is a statement of existence (and through Him all existence came into being) wouldn't we want to approach the question of "who am I" starting from the position of who He is and how we are related to Him. Note the triad expression:

> The Lord: I AM
> The Child: Who Am I?
> The Answer: I am His

Therefore, let's answer the ultimate question in this manner: we are His! His children, His sons and daughters. His people. His servants. We can answer with the simple pronoun: HIS. We are His possession, created and owned by Him, born and guided by Him, reconciled and restored by Him, crafted and commissioned by Him, called and sent by Him. It's all in the context of being His that we find who we really are.

This is great Old Testament theology; for example: the identity of Israel is wrapped up in the concept that they are His people. The horrible converse is found in Hosea where the prophet names one of his children *Lo Ami*, not my people. This prophetic pronouncement would have struck a deep chord of panic in the lives of the Israelites, for there could be no greater disassociation than to no longer be considered "His people." Imagine the relief in Hosea 2:23 when once again the Lord reclaims Israel as "His people." Identity re-established; relationship restored; existence re-assured.

To affirm this possessive relationship is truly an authentic answer for the believer, for the fundamental confession in conversion is a statement of committing our lives totally unto Him. We relinquish our rights to Him, we commend control over to Him, we surrender our lives to His Lordship. We now belong to Him; we are no longer our own, having been bought with a great price. The declaration of the early disciples captured the sentiment in full force: I have been crucified with Christ and it is no longer I who live, but Christ who lives in me.

If, and this is the big "if", we can conclusively and confidently assert this principle in our lives, the impact is profound on our leadership. For now our leadership is not about us, but specifically it is about Him. The determining core of personal success is rooted in our intimate relationship with Him, not the list of our accomplishments or failures. Our first goal as leaders is to be in relationship with Him, and then led by His spirit to "do" the things that matter most to Him. It is the recognition of a spiritual authority and dimension of our lives that supersedes our efforts and accomplishments. Our success is not determined by the trophies on the wall of our personal history, but rather by the ways in which we have fit into a relationship with Him and then His kingdom purpose.

This is incredibly freeing. It doesn't take away personal responsibility, nor does it become fatalistic or deterministic. But it gives us a base and platform for leadership, and the ability to have confidence, guidance, and certainty of perseverance in the face of a buffeting storm. We can tack into the wind because our keel is deep – deep in Him. So, when we strip everything away, we still have Him. And we'll be ok.

The practicality of this is immense. In leadership, we often fall under attack, our organization flounders, or our vision may stagger under the divisive pull of multiple influencers. We may become depressed or discouraged when the numbers and statistics don't follow the amount of effort. The harvest is short lived, or nonexistent in barren soil. If we are "right with God," we can still know, believe, and trust that we are okay, because we are His. If you're a spiritual leader, then you better get this one right. Settle it quickly.

When you have rightly aligned yourself with God, then you can begin to see yourself and who He has crafted you to be. From this point we can then determine the nuances of our personality and skill set as they are imbedded in us by our creator. Think of it as the process of **root, shoot,** and **fruit**.

While the *root* is the core of who we are in Him, the *shoot* is the growing of our personhood, personality, and its unique expression through our skill set and passionate pursuits. The crafting of our God-given abilities are inherent attributes planted by Him when we each are woven in the womb. Genetically we synthesize from our parents, but spiritually God drafts onto our DNA a blue print of our spiritual potential in His kingdom. Hopefully we are nurtured through our home and church to learn how to express those gifts appropriately, but they cannot fully flourish until after we are born again. The physical birth and its gifting doesn't find complete fulfillment without the second birth, the spiritual birth.

Then God grants us a fuller expression as we move into tracks of service and usefulness in His work. With our core or "root" settled we can legitimately see ourselves, by extension, as a husband, pastor, or communicator. These things become an authentic reflection of who we are and moves the concept from a verb to a noun. For instance, *I am a pastor,* not *I pastor a church.* I am a pastor because that's who God has created me to be.

If we genuinely allow this to be fully operational in our lives, then we naturally produce fruit that comes from our core. The third level is the *fruit* where out of our gift-expression comes productivity in His kingdom. Good fruit, by necessity, must be produced by the correlation of the healthy root (relationship) and shoot (maturity and development of His gifting). Out of the overflow and movement of the spirit in the individual's life, these lead to the imminent bearing of produce.

An Old Testament prophet on one occasion taught the listeners about the lack of a solid root and shoot. Though the gardener had attempted to work the soil and plants, the people produced a pitiful crop; he called it "stinky" fruit. It was an indictment against their lack of relationship and maturity of faith. Similarly, we experience little fruit or bad fruit when the soil of our lives is not enriched in a right relationship with God.

Thus being rooted deeply in Christ, and allowing him to be the sustenance of our lives, leads to a healthier *shoot, and* produces good fruit. Each level builds upon the former.

If we look at the total scope of our lives we may discern that we have pinned our hopes on the wrong things and built a self-concept that is singularly rooted in our abilities. Ultimately, we'll find this foundation lacking, or even worse, crumbling and disintegrating. We now know better – based upon the content of this chapter – and can rest more comfortably in an identity that is dependant upon Christ. Even if people see our fruit, our accomplishments, as synonymous with who we are as leaders, we've learned a different process of evaluation.

Hopefully, the more mature will look beyond the fruit (the surface level) and see the core of who we are.

How To Use The *Take Away Realities,* *Core Questions* And *Core Cases*

In each of the chapters, I have included three additional sections that will develop the practical application of the project: ***Take Away Realities, Core Questions*** and ***Core Cases.***

The ***Take Away Realities*** are succinct summary statements of the major concepts of each chapter. In some cases I quote them directly from the text, while occasionally they will be expanded to clarify the thoughts. Use them as a quick overview of the chapter, or a refresher when returning to the book at a later time.

The ***Core Questions*** may be employed in a group setting for general discussion, but you'll also notice that most can be utilized for personal reflection. You may use the queries as a roadmap to help you identify and process specific leadership issues you are confronting. Consider compiling your answers in a separate notebook that you can refer to and develop as a workbook. You'll find it interesting and helpful to look at the larger scope of this book and how your answers reflect your challenges and journey.

If the questions are for group discussion, be aware that some may need to be tweaked to avoid too personal a confrontation or the revealing of confidential material. I urge you to be wise in the dialogue.

The ***Core Cases*** are short narrative summaries of potential leadership issues. It would be impossible to include every nuance of the chapter in which they are embedded, but feel free to draw widely from the subject matter. By nature of their brevity, you'll need to make assumptions from your own experience, or in some cases create additional information that seems reasonable and which allows for fuller discussion. I give you creative license to expand the storyline as needed. Work with the dynamics of the group setting and set out the parameters which you'll allow for each study.

Ultimately, it's my hope that the addition of the **Take Away Realities**, **Core Questions**, and **Core Cases** will help you understand and apply the principles and lessons that you find in nakedLEADERSHIP.

Take Away Realities

- The core of leadership is about who we are rather than what we do. Truly, the first role of the leader is to settle the matter: Who am I?
- The short answer is: I am His. This affirmation becomes the framework from which we operate and provides stability for our personhood.
- We can think of our personhood not as a series of actions, but as the very being of who we are: "I am a pastor," as a noun; not "I pastor a church" as a verb.
- Eventually, success becomes more of an internal judgment, moderated by our relationship with Christ and filtered through the criteria of His purpose in our lives.
- If we root ourselves in Him, then mature in our personhood (shoot), we'll produce good fruit in His kingdom.

Core Questions: Who Am I?

1. How do you normally introduce yourself to others? Write out a typical introduction, then evaluate whether it's more descriptive of what you do compared to who you are.

2. Ask yourself the question: If I strip everything away, who am I at the core? Describe yourself in short statements or single words.

3. Think in terms of your current leadership: do you base your value as a leader on what you've done (past personal history), how well you do your job (present performance), or on who you are (personhood)?

4. List some of your accomplishments. Do those achievements define you? Does your emotional state of healthiness ride up and down based on the list?

5. Evaluate and discuss this statement: If I claim to be a successful pastor when my church explodes in growth, then who am I if my church isn't doing well? Put this into the current dynamic of your leadership role.

6. Write out your agreement or disagreement with this statement: The reality is that leadership is more about "who we are" than "what we do," and that truth sheds light on how we gauge success.

7. If the first task of the leader is to ask, "Who am I," then discuss the framework provided in this chapter of our spiritual relationship to Christ. What impact does that have on our understanding of personal identity? Consider the concepts in the chapter, and

discuss the significance of God's name "I AM" and how that relates to us.

8. Discuss your agreement or not with this statement: The determining core of personal success is rooted in our intimate relationship with Him, not the list of accomplishments or failures.

9. How does the Holy Spirit in you provide for your greatest potential as a leader? Discuss root, shoot, and fruit, and the spiritual DNA infusion that allows our fullest expression to develop. What qualities do you see more fully operational in your life because of your relationship to Christ? What more could develop?

Core Cases: Who Am I?

Case Study 1: The flight from Dallas to Chicago is about four hours long and you are looking forward to talking with the person in the next seat - a well known author that you recognized. After a quick introduction, the author asks what you do. You explain that you are the pastor of a medium-sized church in Chicago, and in the future you, too, have aspirations to write a book. You ask the author to tell about how he launched a writing career. His response included a long list of academics, international ventures, and writing projects. After an hour of hearing his story, you hang your head in dejection and wonder if you could ever do enough to be considered worthy of publication or recognition for your leadership.

> a. What are the initial premises evident in this case concerning personal value and identity?
>
> b. How might the pastor respond in a healthy manner to the list of accomplishments of the author?

Case Study 2: A young seminary graduate recently accepted a call to a large church in Alabama. After buying a home, relocating his family, and setting up his office with an impressive collection of academic books, he now is wondering "what do I do?" His studies in church administration and the leadership books he has read introduced the concepts of managing a staff and leading a church into the process of re-envisioning a future. But the greatest difficulty is his own personal struggles: he's unsure about his capabilities in the pulpit, wrestling with his lack of experience with hospital visitation, and feels severely overwhelmed by the task of long range strategic planning. After several months of inactivity and frustration, he meets with an older, wiser pastor who tells him, "The first thing you need to do is to ask, and then answer, the single most important question." The young man pauses, and asks with a puzzled look on his face, "What is the most important question?" The older pastor reveals the question but the young pastor is puzzled until he takes a three-day personal prayer retreat where things begin to make sense.

    a. Place yourself in this young man's position, how would you respond to the challenge of a new church and having to learn new skills?

    b. This chapter posits that the most important question is, "Who Am I?" Do you agree or not? Explain your answer.

CHAPTER 2

————

The Reveal: Who I Am!

When you pull away the curtain and lower the relational defenses, what glimpse of yourself do you allow people to observe? Do they see the underlying core of your relationship to Him? Most people are not adept at discerning the true spiritual quality of a leader's life, but rather they look at the management style, relational skills, the success of the organization, the fruit of their leadership – or the lack of any of these. They easily confuse personhood and performance and often assign success based on the criterion of accomplishments. It's a judgment call, based on their own perceptions. Some will attempt to categorize and classify you on their terms, and often this is not in your best interest or in flattering words!

Here's the reality: define yourself, or others will define you! This is the second facet of establishing our identity. When we have settled individually who we are, we have a self presentation to make to our world.

> *One of the great failures of mediocre leaders is to let others define who they are.*

The people in our sphere of influence quickly make assessments about who we are - primarily by what we do, the initiatives we propose, how we lead, and the decisions we make. They focus upon outward characteristics and declare they know our leadership styles and predispositions; they judge with certainty our motives. However unfair this may seem, it is a common occurrence.

One of the great failures of mediocre leaders is to let others define who they are. To combat the misrepresentations of others, we must clearly (and often) reiterate the realities, motives, and spiritual inclinations of our hearts. If we have a particular God-given vision, we must articulate and say it unmistakably, and sometimes loudly. If we don't, people will supply a portrait for us, and they will paint us as they want others to see us and in a way that best serves their agenda.

For instance, the common accusation assigned to many pastors who desire for their church to grow is, "all they're concerned about is numbers." Who among us hasn't heard this? It's as though there were something inherently wrong for desiring your church to grow. The naysayers wield this proclamation as means of sabotaging efforts to strategically lead the church forward and to reach more people for Christ. They define the leader as impurely motivated by vain or selfish ambitions; their accusations actually reveal their personal bias and interest in maintaining the status quo.

> It's often more a question of organizational power than organizational purpose.

As we know, it's often more a question of *organizational power* than *organizational purpose*; somehow the naysayers, while acutely focused on our flaws, and who with x-ray vision examine our motives, are narcissistically blind to their own. Yet, their pronouncements take on a spiritual tone that gains ready acceptance, tickling the itching ears of those who desire to maintain the equilibrium of control, contentment, and happiness.

Scripturally, we better be concerned about numbers. Our Lord sure was. Jesus said to His disciples in a parable, "Convince them to come in, so my house may be full." The mandate He gave to the disciples and to the church reminds us of our mission to "Go now and make disciples of all nations ..." Clearly and compellingly, scripture speaks about the importance of reaching people. We've seen occasions where congregations ebb and flow as the "church shuffle" picks up steam at one place - the current hot spot - and then later moves on to another congregation. Our goal, indeed our mandate, is to reach and disciple the unchurched. For this we offer no apology, and if we're sincere and faithful to this cause, our churches should grow, burgeon, maybe even explode. To the detractors, conversely, our desire for growth seems showy or ambitious; thus, they question our motives, publicly and critically. If we allow their message to supersede the reality of our motives, then we'll lose the battle through a lack of self definition.

I'm convinced that we have to be our own advocates, advocates of truth, not advocates with personal vindictiveness or justification. We have a responsibility to keep truth and transparency in the forefront of every spiritual leadership process in the church. Nowhere is that more critical than the leader speaking truth about himself or herself.

Sounds a little like self promoting, but if you don't declare it, they'll make it up! Their fabrications are far worse than the things you express about yourself. The mind has an incredible capacity to fill in the gaps of information with wild thoughts. It's easy for someone to subtly drop hints and let the imagination of the individual run with it. A nuanced half truth will become a major accusation in the mind of one who is willing and primed to believe the worst.

The scriptures have a word for it: the *yetzer* of the Old Testament, more commonly known as the imagination of the mind. It's a God-given ability to let reason fly and thoughts soar, but when coupled with mankind's sinful nature, it often bends toward believing the worst rather than the best.

For instance, I thoroughly enjoy watching movies, but I consume a novel because my mind can create the world of fiction with the hints of information given by the author. This is probably true for us all: the use of vivid phrases or subtle word choices, coupled with syntactic complexity nudge the reader toward constructing the visual world of the novel in our heads. Oh, how our minds race. Long before Peter Jackson portrayed the stunning landscapes of the "Lord of the Rings," we had already conjured images of the Shire, the mines of Moria, the fields of Rohan, the forests of the Ents, and the tower of the dark lord. Thankfully, Jackson did an incredible job of fleshing out those images!

If we allow our detractors, or de-visioneers, (to pun the word division) to cast allusions or cleverly influence people by what they say and how they say it, without a truth-speaking-answer from us, the construct of people's mind will move toward the negative and will build resistance to the vision. We must use our positional voice in leadership and drop hints, paint our own pictures of a different future, or delineate strategically our thoughts and hopes. If we fill in the blanks for our people, they will be less likely to fill them in for us.

Nowhere is that more true than in introducing motives into the discourse and storyline of your leadership. We desire for people to believe the best about us. Over a period of time, as we consistently live out our character and integrity, we attempt to build the impression in people's minds that deters the false *yetzer*. Yet, in reality we know that people may hastily change their opinions about us and mistrust builds rapidly. I'm often amazed at how quickly and easily people believe the worst about someone. They see an action they don't understand, consequences of a decision they don't agree with, or assumptions and unfair correlations that cause them to doubt. This results in an erosion of trust, and especially, suspicion of our motives.

Right motives are one of several areas in which we must learn to be transparent. We cannot afford to keep them close to the vest. Motives must be backed up by a consistent demonstration of humility and consistency in our message. Appropriate motives, reinforced by humility and by surrendering to the Lord's will, are a defensive mechanism against antagonists.

> *Motives must be backed up by a consistent demonstration of humility and consistency in our message.*

People will often project their fears into presumed motives, assuming a worse case scenario and interpolating your decisions to be insensitive to them. This compels us to speak clearly of our motives, which when coupled with our dreams and visions, can provide a clear path to a new future.

Another component that infuses power into motive is passion, which reveals the deepest emotive quality of our thoughts. When passion is communicated and observed, such as in a sermon, most people translate this into sincerity (more on passion later). When people understand our motives, know the passion that drives our motives, and subsequently agree with our motives, a powerful unleashing of energy and momentum can be accomplished.

All in all, we must acknowledge the second step in the process of self-identification is to establish ourselves unambiguously to our organizations and followers. Despite the attempts of people to disqualify or discredit you as a leader, you can overcome false or inaccurate perceptions by your consistent presentation. Leader – define yourself!

Take Away Realities

- Define yourself before others define you. It is your responsibility to "self present" your leadership.
- One of the greatest failures in mediocre leaders is to let others define them.
- Consistently remind the members of the realities of the organizational purpose.
- Clarify and reassert your personal motives.
- People sometimes accuse leaders of ulterior motives as means of holding onto organizational power.
- Be an advocate of truth and transparency in the process of spiritual leadership of the church.
- People will often project their own fears onto our motives and assume worse case scenarios; therefore, it is necessary to speak clearly of our motives.

Core Questions for The Reveal

1. Using short statements, list and then describe how others possibly perceive you. How accurate would you consider their assessments to be, and why or why not?

2. Consider the statement: define yourself, or others will define you! Relate some of your attempts to define yourself and ask how effective you were in doing so?

3. Can you remember a time when you were defined in a way that was frustrating or degrading to you? Describe this assault and the "yetzer" of the accusations.

4. Why or how could organizational power and organizational purpose be at odds? Is it possible for them to be compatible; why or why not?

5. If you are an advocate of truth concerning your motives and transparent in the leadership process, you may have to "self promote." Is this comfortable for you to do? What methods could you use that are appropriate for your leadership profile and personality?

6. Consider your current leadership decisions and evaluate the motives that are attached to them. Did you make the decisions using right motives? Reflect on different outcomes if you operated from different motives. Could your motives stand the test of exposure and revelation? Is there a mentor or peer group that could be a sounding board for an honest discussion of motives?

Core Cases for The Reveal

Case Study 1: Pastor Don Jameston has led the First Methodist Church of Medlin for six years through several significant transitions including staff expansion and schedule changes. The most recent endeavor includes a twelve month study of long range needs, with a concluding report and recommendations to be presented at the next business meeting. He almost immediately hears of opposition to several of the initiatives outlined in the long range proposal. One individual in particular has brought to light previous conversations, where the pastor had talked openly and freely about things he would like to see happen in the future of First Church. The opponent has taken earlier comments out of context and is using them to promote the idea that the Pastor had already made up his mind about what needed to be done, long before the Long Range Planning Committee started their work.

    a. In the context of this chapter what might the pastor do to correct the perception created by the opponent?

    b. Using the case study, what elements of "organizational power" and "organizational purpose" are in operation here?

Case Study 2: In a number of committee meetings, opponents have consistently complained that the organization's leader doesn't listen to their suggestions and input and has isolated himself from the members. They claim he is autocratic and is pushing his own agenda, and his programming proposals will take away some of their responsibilities (read authority). They have sent a letter to a number of members with a list of the faults they see in the leader. Their hope is to discredit his proposals, limit his leadership, and re-assert their authority. The board of the non-profit has called a meeting to discuss the actions of the leader.

    a. Consider the initial theme of this chapter, define yourself or others will define you, and apply it to this case study. What might the leader do to combat the perception that the opponents are trying to create.

    b. How might the leader better reveal his own personal motives as compared to the intentions of the opposition group?

Mark W. Gregory

CHAPTER 3

The Prestige: What is Leadership?

A popular movie, *The Prestige*, portrayed the rivalry between two magicians (illusionists) who each sought for larger renown than the other. Their acts developed greater drama and flair, and the point when the illusionists awed the crowd became known as the prestige. This was the moment that the magic man held the audience in his hand, an instant when the crowd was captivated. It was the apex of *buy in*, *believability*, and willingness to go with the illusionist to that mysterious place of wonder.

On an organizational level, there are similar occasions of *buy in*, when followers and members invest in the purpose of the group. It can be a magical moment when the hopes of the leader, the goals of the organization, and the desires of the people coalesce into a concerted effort and movement. This is when the core of the leader and his or her motives are truly put to the test, because our personal interests must be subservient to the future needs of our people. Knowing that we've faithfully heard from God, we're willing to lead these people to a new spiritual place - a place determined by God, not by our own reason or strategy.

There have been so many definitions of leadership over the years that it appears there is little consensus of what it really is. *Leadership is our ability to influence others* is a popular mantra: this is true. *Leadership doesn't happen unless people follow* or *Leadership is more art than science:* these statements also have merit. They each encapsulate important facets of successful leadership and truly reflect different aspects of the function of guiding a group of people.

My own understanding of leadership has wandered through the mazes of books, articles, and conferences, where each new theory is accorded, "Yes, that's it!" But when I place myself in the leadership mix and correlate it to the practitioner's role, I've reduced it to the specific context of spiritual or benevolent leadership – assuming that authentic leadership always has a beneficent role. To have this positive impact, there is a basic assumption about the person who is leading, that he or she is not a self-serving, ambition-wielding, and people-trampling person. There are implications for the people that are involved in the process of follower-ship, that ultimately the place the leader desires to take them has merit and would be worthy of the journey. When I compact all the dynamics of the process into a sequential pattern I end up with a healthy cycle of leader, follower, and end point. Here's how it looks to me:

> Leadership is when *a person of character takes a committed people to a place of change.*

Let me be clear: there have been many people who have been horrific leaders – leaders nonetheless, but not examples that we would emulate or promulgate their practices. For the purposes of this study, we're talking primarily about spiritual leadership which has positive consequences in people's lives – and subsequently, leadership that moves people in a healthy and benevolent direction.

A Person of Character

Because we're seeking a helpful outcome for people's lives, character counts. Character is the baseline of trust which is critical for any effective leader. The trust we build in relationships with others is a part of the process of transparency (I'll explain more fully in Chapter 15). Also, the scriptures remind us of the godly character that correlates to perseverance, longevity, and hope – essentials for leadership.

It is asserted that leaders can compartmentalize their lives and have integrity in one area but not in another. I've typically observed that there is a bleed over from places of weakness that impact the whole person in spite of protests otherwise. It seems incredulous to think that character values, or lack of values, in one part wouldn't affect another. Biblically and psychologically we're more of an integrated whole than fragmented parts, and one of the goals of the individual is to work toward a congruency of these facets of life.

Character is also a determinate of direction: bad character is composed of certain traits that include selfishness, self-promotion, and self-directed ambition. If one's character is bent toward, let's say, self preservation, then the leader will manipulate, leverage, and lead an organization to promulgate or perpetuate the leader's position. Everything that he or she does has a top priority of guarding their power status, prestige, and control. This may be an area that pastors fall prey to easily. Much of church politics is about power and control, and it is simple for the pastor or leader to set up systems to keep him in the power seat. By slight of hand, diplomacy, and manipulation (sometimes justified improperly by poor spiritual motives), he tries to squash opposition or even constructive critique, or at best consistently builds a base of support to keep himself intact.

The end result of such maneuvering is contrary to the model of Christ, where leadership is service and beneficent driven. Rather than safeguarding our position, we're to be more concerned about nurturing other's connection to God's will. In his book on spiritual leadership, Henry Blackaby correctly turned the tables. The role of the spiritual leader is to align people with God's will, and let me add to this: not to force them into our own ambitious agendas.

From character and integrity, personal authority springs forth. (I'll present more on positional and personal authority later). At this point, we'll acknowledge that the strongest base of personal authority is established when a leader builds respect by his spiritual composure, sensitivity

> *Before people will follow a vision they believe in, they must be willing to believe in the leader of the vision.*

to the needs of his organization, and the depth of his personal character. Before people will follow a vision they believe in, they must be willing to believe in the leader of the vision.

Committed People

The second dynamic of the definition relates to the people who participate in the church or organization. True: leaders must have followers - and the best followers are those who buy into the vision and direction, irrespective of whether volunteer or paid. Admittedly, you often have more leverage and incentive with those who are paid employees, but they, too, must believe in the vision of the organization as communicated by the leaders. To assess your people, consider a number of levels beginning with the passive outside observers, to the casual and infrequent participants, to the highest level of regular contributing team members.

We made a foundational shift several years ago when we established a totally new concept of servant ministry at Calvary Baptist Church. We introduced and launched the church without the typical office of deacon or the use of committees – both well entrenched and universally accepted institutions in church life. Essentially, we removed a middle layer of the hierarchy and sought to put more people closer to the ministries of the church, not insulated from them. This increased the potential for people to get their hands into the dirt work of church life. Subsequently they became more involved in decision making and providing feedback on the systems that were working and those that were not. We also discovered that they are more likely to "buy in" when they were a part of process and could help shape the direction.

From a biblical position, how did we justify this? Simple. We combined the scriptural concept of deacons (which is servanthood) and the administrative function of committees and developed a system of Servant Teams. Almost every form of direct ministry at Calvary is conducted through teams: the pastoral team, ministry leadership teams, or servant teams. In particular, to be on a servant team, you're not elected in the traditional method of deacon selection, you volunteer. The ministries are not restricted to persons who are elected for a term, but are staffed by people who feel a burden for a certain area of ministry in the life of the church. Through this process, we are able to increase the number of people who are involved in the work of our Church. It is necessary for leadership functions to be staffed by those who are significantly invested in the church, so there are certain teams and positions that are filled by appointment rather than by volunteering – these do require membership.

Committed people are those who *know the vision, trust the leader,* and whose *personal spiritual journey aligns with the long-term goals of the organization.* This means that the leader has done his work in sharing and casting the vision, and it is one that participants know to be worthwhile. It infers they are willing to follow the leader because there is a level of trust that the leader cares about the organizational purpose and also

> *Committed people are those who know the vision, trust the leader, and whose personal spiritual journey aligns with the long-term goals of the organization.*

is concerned about the organizational "people." If these things line up, you increase the capacity for investment and involvement from the people. If their journey coincides with the direction the organization is moving, they will often go further than a brief intersection of interests and a passing commitment.

Occasionally, I lead a class on leadership at a local university; among the many questions I receive, a recurring theme is, "how do you motivate your people." This is an appropriate topic whether working with paid personnel or with volunteers. With paid personnel, the best employee is one who really understands the organizational goals, believes in them, trusts the leadership, and (let's not diminish this part) who has a financial incentive to do a good job. The check and balance of routine performance reviews or the on-the-hoof corrective comments are appropriate means of managing the productivity of the employee. I've frequently discerned that there are two beneficial facets of paid personnel compared to non-paid. One is time. Generally the paid person has a more consistent and dedicated schedule applied toward the accomplishment of a goal. The second is follow-through. While many volunteers are top notch and perform adequately, the leverage of remuneration can more likely guarantee complete follow through. On both counts, though, the expectations of the leader must be communicated and clearly reinforced. If people know what is expected before they commit, they are much more likely to follow through.

We can't omit the spiritual element to motivation. In this case the church has the greatest incentive of all – a spiritual return, an influential harvest, and an eternal reward. I'm consistently pleased and appreciative of how much people in the church give and contribute to the cause of Christ. Deepening and developing the spiritual life of your members can be an appropriate focus of your leadership; even in non-church environments, leading your employees spiritually as a tertiary goal can help refine the organizational purpose.

Place of Change

What about the "place of change?" Change is difficult and nowhere is it more precipitous than in the church. Here, our die is cast and our bounty won. The place of change is an objective future point that pulls us, or in some cases pushes us; it is an identifiable spot that collectively we want to go to.

> *Identify the spot, celebrate the arrival, and refocus on the next spot. Keep pushing the spot further out.*

Change often comes with a high cost, and is effected because of great pain or due to huge incentives. But ultimately in most people's minds, leadership will be judged by the arrival at a predetermined destination. Unfair or not, this is a reality and often is the designation of success. I'm willing to say this is true in many cases, but there's another level of success that is more about the journey toward change rather than the arrival. The good news is that the journey is often as important, if not more important, than the arrival. The journey brings transformation of individual lives, and often morphs the organization into a new mode of healthier operation. This is a good thing.

Regardless, for the leader, an important objective is to identify the spot, celebrate the arrival, and refocus on the next spot. Keep pushing the spot further out, not to the degree that people become discouraged, but just far enough ahead to keep your people moving. (There's a whole chapter devoted to managing change.) The first and most important part is to mark that spot on the wall. There's an old saying, *don't look where you don't want to go*, which I've re-qualified in positive terms, *look where you want to go*.   To rephrase it, determine that place that is a picture of what you want to look like. Focus on where your vision takes you.

Practically, it has to be a place that the majority of your people agree is worthy of the effort that will be required. If you can't take most of them with you, you might ask, is this where our organization needs to go? It may be that you're not matched well with the organization, and your interests, passions, and vision are out of step with the nature of the organization. It may be disastrous to attempt a DNA substitution.

Let's also acknowledge that not everyone will see eye to eye about where you're headed. Sometimes the leader has a larger perspective than the members of the organization; then bringing the vision and the people together becomes the task. Yet, be cautious about compromise and synthesis of two perspectives/visions unless it enlarges the vision and maintains the direction. Negotiating and compromising could potentially lead to a diluting of the vision; even a few degrees of divergence can lead the organization to a totally different place, one that drastically misses the mark. The leader has to maintain constancy of direction while allowing and encouraging input - a balancing act at best. Occasionally, the only reason some people make it to the end of the journey is because they trust the leader. So, the end starts with you.

So, the place of change has to be *believable*, *attainable*, and *worthy of pursuit*. This is where religious organizations

> *The place of change has to be believable, attainable, and worthy of pursuit.*

have a great advantage, because we believe in the inherent value of our calling to minister in this world. And if people truly capture the passion to reach people for Christ, they're more willing to endure or tolerate change. I recently received a wonderful note from a member who expressed how the Lord had changed her heart and perspective about contemporary Christian music as she thought about the ultimate goal of reaching the younger generation for Christ. We know that for many churches, this has been a bloody battlefield.

I also remember an earlier time when I encountered significant resistance to the theme of an organizational change: "Whatever it takes." Now, after some years of maturing as a leader, I'm better able to understand the concerns they raised. Yet, I am still puzzled by the unwillingness to reach for the goals of soul winning and outreach that we'd laid out. In that context, the organization failed to adopt a long range plan that had been researched and developed for a year or more – the only time I've known of a plan that did not pass approval of important steps for the future.

The Scope of the Definition

What does this definition do for us? First it highlights that each of us should settle in our own hearts how we see and understand leadership. We've got to find our own way of "inflicting" it upon ourselves and remaining true to our conclusions. Second, by determining the definition, we're setting the parameters of how we'll gauge ourselves (notice I didn't say "how we succeed," though there are overtones of quantitative measurement that can be applied). Last, by reaching our own definition, or by adopting another's – such as mine – we've set the foundation for how we'll proceed. You have to start somewhere, and a thorough definition is a great place to begin.

Take Away Realities

- Develop or adopt a definition of leadership and use it as means for understanding how you lead and where you are leading. You may use this book's definition as a point of departure: *Leadership is when a person of character takes committed people to a place of change.*
- In benevolent leadership, character counts.
- Committed people are those who *know the vision, trust the leader,* and whose *personal spiritual journey aligns with the long-term goal of the organization.*
- Before people will follow a vision they believe in, they must be willing to believe in the leader of the vision.
- Determine the spot to shoot for, and ensure it is worthy of the quest. Identify the spot, celebrate the arrival, and focus on the next spot. Keep pushing the spot further out.
- The place of change has to be *believable, attainable,* and *worthy of pursuit.*

Core Questions for The Prestige:
What is Leadership?

1. Have there been moments of "buy in" in your leadership journey, times when it's clear that people are on board and willing to follow? Reflect on what precipitated the "buy in."

2. Write out your favorite leadership definition and describe why it appeals to you. Does that definition stand the test of time?

3. The definition presented in this chapter, "when a person of character takes committed people to a place of change," introduces three distinct levels. Beginning with the first level and assuming we're talking about benevolent leadership, do you believe that character counts? Describe your reasoning for agreeing or disagreeing.

4. The chapter discusses compartmentalization of character actions. Do you believe that it's possible for a character flaw in one area to not affect another? Why or why not?

5. Describe the difference between personal authority and positional authority? Which has greater merit for a spiritual leader?

6. Reflect on whether you agree with this statement: Before people will follow a vision they believe in, they must be willing to believe in the leader of the vision.

7. In light of the concept: "Committed people are those who *know the vision, trust the leader,* and whose *personal spiritual journey aligns with the long-term goals of the organization*" list the elements that lead

to greater commitment from the members of an organization.

8. In leadership, how important is it to identify the spot or place of change? What are the elements that help qualify the place of change?

9. Discuss the cost of the journey to that spot. Will, or should, everyone go with you to that place? Are you prepared to lose people on the journey?

10. Write out modified definition of leadership that best matches you at this point.

A Core Case for Leadership Defined

A new leader has just begun work for his organization. Though his previous employment was as an associate and he had little leadership experience, he's now ready to give it a try. After reading through a number of books on leadership, he is not satisfied with the simple definitions presented. He is preparing to lead a group of key members through an initial planning session and wants to explain leadership using a new definition: leadership is when a person of character takes a committed people to a place of change. He presents the three facets in the concepts of **person**, **people** and **place** as the model to identify future strategies. In their first meeting they evaluate the current state of the organization and begin brainstorming about the things that need to be done. The leader wants to systematize their discussions:

   a. How might he use this structure (person, people, place) to identify and develop strategies?

Use the following questions to further refine your answers:

   b. Who is the primary leader of the organization? Does the leader have the trust of the organizational members? Identify key leaders who might be instrumental in the process of change.

c. Have the people of the church or organization bought into the vision and direction of the leader? What steps might be taken to increase the general level of interest and participation? Is there a unity in the organization? Has the church developed a culture of change?

d. Is there a clear and well-delineated vision? Project future end points as examples.

e. Evaluate potential end points using the question, is the place of change believable, attainable, and worthy of pursuit?

CHAPTER 4

A New Reality: Re-Defining Success

The sequence of the first three chapters leads naturally to the following issue: we've defined leadership, but how do we gauge success in leadership? What does success look like? Can we use the same markers that the corporate world uses to identify a successful organization or leader? Should we? The short answer: a resounding "No!" Markers and benchmarks are important tools for evaluative purposes, but the equivocation of positive results/return and success is too simple a paradigm. The reality of an organization such as a church is that spiritual dynamics and movements are not tied to numbers. The benchmarks must include qualitative criterion, not just quantitative (as discussed later in this chapter).

The problem is fairly evident and resonates clearly with many leaders who find themselves in healthy ministries that produce good fruit, but the results of their labor are not found in numbers. They are easily tempted to feel, let's say, less than successful. We've set them up for a defeat by considering only one dimension of success, and many fall prey to its entrapment! Ironically, an Australian prison ship by the name of Success provides an intriguing analogy of ensnarement, with the similar result of stagnation. Built around 1840 as a merchant ship, Success was partially abandoned at Melbourne in the early 1850's after its crew fled to the Australian gold fields. It was then purchased to serve as a prison ship since jails were full. Moored and non-sailable, it sat as a hulk until it was used as a storage vessel. Only years later did it sail again, but only as a floating museum. The name of the ship, Success, hardly correlates to its inglorious use.

We often build our lives around "success" believing that if we could attain a certain measure of financial compensation, personal recognition, organizational growth, then everything would be perfect. But in reality we become caught in the striving for triumph and begin rotting from the inside out, resting in stagnant water. To reach goals only to discover that they weren't satisfying is indicative of the seductive trap of success. This is the circle: if unsatisfied at one level, you must reach to the next to get it. When that doesn't satisfy, you reach again. It's an unending cycle of aspiration. Truly, this doesn't reflect a healthy viewpoint for success.

From a personal perspective, I'm in the one of the most successful churches of my pastoral tenure. It's the healthiest of virtually any organization in which I have been a part, and our journey as a church has been rich and blessed. We are ten years old, own forty acres of property, with a first phase facility that equals many longer term, established churches. We are in a community that is growing, and yes, our church has burgeoned to a "medium-sized" congregation. Given these factors, it might seem odd to say that I sometimes feel unsuccessful. My moments of deprecation or frustration are almost always geared toward the quantitative side of the evaluation curve; especially if I compare myself, or our church, to other churches and leaders. What a heavy and unnecessary load if I allow myself to persist under that criterion!

In Christian circles we have done no less than glamorize the mega church pastors of our time as rock stars, where success is usually defined in terms of the quantity of people who attend their churches. We then extrapolate positive numerical trends as symptomatic of the leadership traits of success. We subsequently contend that those leaders have unique personal characteristics or qualities that we should emulate. We unintentionally affirm this thought when those same leaders show up at conferences or in articles about any number of church growth topics, as if there is some hidden or inexplicable information that they can impart and that should replicate.

Hardly, if ever, do you see a church growth conference where the speakers are from very small churches. We might give tacit affirmation to the faithfulness of these "mini" or "medi" church pastors, but when it comes to who we want to hear, give us the big guns. Give us the leaders who have reached the stars, who have conquered the untapped potential of the lost world, and who have regularly packed the auditoriums.

It's a dangerous place emotionally for a "mega" leader in this position since it's tempting to believe the press and develop a skewed perspective of self. We treat these speakers and leaders as though there's something special about them – and sometimes they treat themselves that way, also. I read a tweet recently that challenges this risky perspective well: "What if we treated rock stars like regular people, and regular people like rock stars." Do these pastors deserve our adulation? No. Are there things we can learn from them? Absolutely yes! So, let's look at them from the right point of view and with the appropriate corrective lenses.

There are many wonderful, creative, innovative, and cutting edge mega churches. Unlike most naysayers, I think there's merit in the resources and reach of the larger churches. What made those churches what they are? A lot of hard work, significant sacrifice, spiritual intuition and smart thinking. Add to that fortitude, the blessing of good timing, strategic location, and certainly the movement of the Holy Spirit; which often results in one visible sign of success - numbers. Did you catch the last phrase – "one visible sign"? Numbers may be a symptom of success, but conversely numbers don't always predicate success. There is a hazardous temptation to think of a crowd as an indication of success, but the greater question is whether we create a culture of faith, and faithfulness. Some larger organizations may appear successful by the sheer mass that flocks to participate, while inwardly there may be secrets, sin, and fundamental characteristics that lead to a precipitous fall.

What about the people who are trudging in the trenches of the majority of churches: moderate-sized churches in medium-sized towns that are declining in numbers and their congregations reflect that same trend. Are these churches somehow not blessed, or cursed? We may not say it, but we may wonder: "What's wrong with that church?" "There must be something going on there, or else they would be growing." Certainly, there are churches that are small due to the ineffectiveness of a ministry team or a dysfunctional membership, but in reality many smaller churches may be very successful in their ministries. This is spot on, especially if we understand the true biblical context of success, which is related to faithfulness.

I'm going to state what should be self-evident: size does not automatically equal success. I contend that success can be found in the myriad of medium-sized to small congregations where the pastor and the leaders are faithfully executing the ministry of Christ. To help us all get a better handle on how to gauge it, I'm proposing a different paradigm, one based on qualitative and quantitative means and undergirded by the most dominant biblical theme of success: Faithfulness.

The Biblical Baseline of Success: Success is not determined by numbers but by integrity, character, and faithfulness to the ministry where God has called you. The biblical model of success is always faithfulness: faithfulness to the call the Lord has placed on one's life, and faithfulness in the journey. It is the plumb line

> *The biblical model of success is always faithfulness ... Faithfulness is the plumb line to which all other aspects of evaluation must be applied.*

to which all other aspects of evaluation must be applied. Among the many prophets of the Old Testament, the Lord spoke through Amos to remind his people of their aptitude to detour from His standard and His way. His message incorporated the analogy of the plumb line or measuring line, which became the means to compare their wanderings and how far afield they had gone. The plumb line is a tool by which you gauge the straightness of a wall and the accuracy of construction. For Amos's preaching, it symbolized how obedient or disobedient the people of God were to the standards that He set for them – thus it became a word picture concerning their inadequacy of relationship with Him. Ultimately, faithfulness is the greatest gauge of our lives, ministries, and organizations.

The parable of the talents is particularly instructive in exploring this paradigm. Christ placed the parable in the larger context of the kingdom illustrations: Matthew 24, which reveals the signs of the end of the age, and Matthew 25, with its parables of the ten virgins, the ten talents, and the sheep and the goats. Both chapters draw attention not just to the events of the end times, but to the manner in which the people of the kingdom will be judged for their kingdom contributions. The pinnacle of the presentation is the parable of the talents which details the measure against which faithfulness is judged.

The story unfolds with three persons each given a number of talents (remember that the talents are a financial measurement – a very specific gauge of value). The first was given five talents, the second received two talents, and the last was given one talent. The first person invested and doubled the money; the second person, though given less, also doubled the money; while the last man hid the money and returned only the amount given him. The master responded identically to two of the servants: "You acted well, good and faithful servant. Since you were faithful in little things, I will give you responsibility over great things."

What's critical to note is that the two men were not judged differently on the basis of the amount of money they were given; they both received equal approval from the master. The measure, or plumb line, was how faithful they were with what they had – in essence, a qualitative not quantitative judgment. The master then follows the initial statement with a follow-up concerning their capacity for even greater things since they have been faithful in these first matters. This echoes the principle given by Christ that if we desire to be faithful in much we must first be faithful in little, for the small things precede and undergird the larger things.

The relative nature of the success was based on their faithfulness. Now recall the third servant who did nothing with his amount. Though he didn't lose it, he squandered the potential inherent in his gift and was unfaithful to the tasks of the master. The master strongly condemned his lack of initiative and failure to contribute to the kingdom. While the overtones of the parable convey qualitative and quantitative criteria, both are set in the context of faithfulness to the call of the master. This commitment to the call is the common denominator that keeps all other measurements in proper balance and perspective.

> *Faithfulness in the small things precede and undergird the larger things.*

To reinforce this paradigm further, note the chapter of faith in Hebrews Eleven. The narrative begins with a roster of the faithful, most of which we would easily gauge as successful or blessed in some manner: Abel, Enoch, Noah, Abraham, Moses, and others. These individuals knew the blessing of God and saw the beginnings of the history of Israel. But the list doesn't stop there! The chapter describes other spiritual heroes of the ancient times, including many others who were faithful under adversity, persecution, and even death. They are just as important in the list and just as instructive for us. Their faithfulness did not correspond to blessing, but to persistence in spite of difficulty. Note the following adversities as recorded from Verses 35 and following. They were:

- Tortured
- Mocked
- Flogged
- Chained
- Imprisoned
- Stoned
- Sawn into
- Poorly clothed in sheepskins and goatskins
- Persecuted
- Wanderers without a home

This secondary list reflects the opposite of our typical definition of success. These individuals received recognition not because of their power, status, or possessions, but rather for their rejection of them. Their faithfulness to the core ideologies of their God sets in place a different standard by which we live and by which we are judged.

Qualitative and Quantitative: To expand a revised paradigm for success, consideration of two other elements is essential. Balancing these two, qualitative and quantitative, requires the common denominator that I've described above, but each can provide a perspective that helps assess personal (or organizational) stasis or progress. There's nothing wrong with looking closely at where we stand on that continuum.

The Qualitative Call: A qualitative analysis starts with the fundamental purpose of the individual or the organization; in ministry we often state this as a personal or church mission statement. But looking more specifically at the individual facet, there is a "call" or "commission" that usually drives us in a direction to fulfill a purpose. The baseline of this call then becomes the means whereby we ascertain the qualitative components and then judge how effective we are in our roles. If we were to summarize this principle, we might say it like this: success is when you faithfully do what you're called to do!

For those who serve outside the church in a secular venue, don't let this terminology throw you. You may not think of this in spiritual terms, but every person has a "calling" and can fulfill specific purposes. The concept of calling originates in scripture from the Greek word KALEO, *to call, invite,* or *to name,* and is rendered at least once as vocation in the noun form, KLESIS. Calling is an invitation or naming of an individual to a manner of life or a pursuit in life. In times past, we saw something of this when people took a surname as an indication of their vocation: smithing became Smith, coopering became Cooper. The Latin originally incorporated this concept using the term VOCARE, from which we derive the English term vocation. In essence, an individual's vocational pursuit may be a God-given calling, especially if that person understands the spiritual dynamics of the work environment being a place of ministry. By extension, the leader fulfills a unique role by guiding and shaping the culture to achieve the goals and purpose of the organization.

For us, then, as leaders, one aspect of gauging our leadership is to evaluate how true we have been to the calling placed on our lives. Are we still tracking along the trajectory that the call put us on? As a pilot, I'm required to make small adjustments to my heading in order to stay on course to my destination. Things such as offset headwinds or gyro deviation can slightly veer me off by a few degrees; so, I'm constantly navigating to ensure that I arrive at the correct airport. To put this in practical terms related to my ministry, if I have been called to preach, am I being faithful to that calling? Am I putting the appropriate effort into the development of my preaching preparation that promotes the spiritual health and growth of my church? Is what my church family receives from me each week the quality that they deserve and the respect that the scripture engenders?

There's an old story about a farmer who attends church one Sunday, and though the attendance was low the preacher fanned the flames of exhortation in the usual amount of intensity. Upon greeting the parson at the back of the sanctuary at the end of the sermon, the farmer explained that when feeding his cattle, he doesn't drop the whole load if they don't all show up. While humorously appreciated for its witty point, the joke misses the faithfulness of the pastor preaching just as sincerely for one as for a hundred, or to a hundred as compared to a thousand, or a thousand to ten thousand. While at conferences, we hear inspiring sermons from well-known speakers from larger churches, but I have a hunch that the greatest sermons are probably being delivered each week to small congregations where they are heard by only a handful of people. Those sermon notes are filed in a cabinet and probably never to be retrieved. The pastor launches the process of study for the next sermon, knowing that only a handful will ever hear it as well. Faithfulness to the call means we deliver the highest quality sermon regardless of the number in the audience.

What if you're an educational administrator? In the classes I've had the privilege to teach at the local university, a number are returning educators who want to excel in their administrative skills. It's a great calling to infuse into the educational system the highest quality of your effort that has life long impact on teachers and students. What if you are the leader of a not-for-profit social ministry? Your calling is sacrosanct and faithfulness to your calling will be the means by which you are judged. The principle applies to the larger dynamic of an organization. Is it fulfilling its purpose? This is a qualitative assessment, based purely upon calling, life mission, or organizational purpose and the level that we are staying on track to be true to that purpose.

The Qualitative Character: Another qualitative perspective also relates to the concept of character. Scriptures places a high value on the integrity of the individual, specifically godly character. There have been revelations in recent years of the lack of

> *Among the many vocations, Christian leaders must maintain the greatest possible standard, even avoiding the appearance of evil.*

character and integrity of a few high profile Christian

leaders. Among the many vocations, Christian leaders must maintain the greatest possible standard, even avoiding the appearance of evil. One of the Old Testament words for character and integrity is TAM, which at the root means *wholeness* or *completion.* When an individual fully integrates godliness, purity, and integrity into their lives and maintains it over the course of their lives, we affirm that they have reached a level of success completely irrespective of power, status, accomplishments, or possessions. This is without question – success! I was thrilled when one of my sons commented on the need to talk to me about a deep theological question, which to me was an acknowledgement that I had something to contribute to his life. I was blessed when the other son commented about the godly character that he recognized and wanted to emulate. One of the heroes of the New Testament said it best: I have fought the good fight, I have finished the race. This is a qualitative benchmark!

The Qualitative Culture: The third qualitative perspective is based on the unique organizational culture the leader has been able to cultivate. Creating a healthy corporate environment is a worthy goal and is direct evidence of a successful leader. Some organizations are known by an informal work-place, a cutting edge mentality, or by any number of identifiers. But systemic functionality of the organization can create healthiness,

> *Success occurs when an organization achieves a level of healthiness that allows it to pursue an appropriate calling with its particular set of goals, and thereby accomplishes those goals in a manner consistent with its character.*

such as: the openness to dialogue about issues or problems; hierarchical transparency that allows interaction between leaders, management and employees; encouraging participation and investment "buy in"; developing a system of caring for employees and volunteers that is based on genuine compassion.

A paradigm for success can be found in the following statement: success occurs when an organization achieves a level of healthiness that allows it to pursue an appropriate calling with its particular set of goals, and thereby accomplishes those goals in a manner consistent with its character.

Qualitative Personal Relevancy: Success on the personal level may be relative and more dependant upon personal goals or relational attributes. There is a target goal or line that's appropriate to hit, but for each person or organization that benchmark is different. When we designed our martial arts ministry at Calvary, we decided two things: we would build our program differently than most schools which expected a minimum of three days a week for class participation. This level of attendance was unrealistic for us, in that, our program initially was designed for professionals, business persons, or active families, who could only give one day a week. Remember also that we were not driven by the need to financially sustain a level of income to fund capital overhead. We saw this school as a ministry. Secondly, while there would be the some standard benchmarks as in most programs, we considered the progress of the individual on a scale congruent with their own potential rather than an aggregate and sometimes unreachable standard. In other words, you don't have to be a Bruce Lee to obtain a black belt. We were able to set goals and establish criteria based on the abilities and aptitudes of the students. It's a system that has been in place now for a number of years – and it works quite well, thank you.

Realistically, success must be more measurable than a sliding scale, but on some level success does reside in the eye of the beholder. And that's where the person must set goals for his organization that are congruent to the purpose and appropriate for evaluation.

Quantitative Success: At some point it's okay to set quantitative goals and use them for determining progress. If they are balanced correctly by the quality and health of the organization, and they are underscored by the measure of faithfulness to the calling and purpose, then by all means, factor them into the equation. But, the equation works best when you don't reverse the order. Often an organization that grows too rapidly numerically will outstrip its health potential and ends up deviating from its purpose.

Carefully decide which quantitative factors are worthy of review and will give an accurate picture of where the organization stands. These benchmarks can be a huge "shot in the arm" for the team, and additionally, achieving certain numerical goals is one of the building blocks of momentum. In organizational terms, when you get a group or company rolling, its sheer mass creates movement, and more movement creates more mass. It can be a cyclical experience at times and is rewarding if

> *Carefully decide which quantitative factors are worthy of review and will give an accurate picture of where the organization stands.*

placed in the proper context. For the church, the temptation is to take credit for the growth as though we've done something special, when in reality the growth occurred as a result of many dynamics.

What might be considered legitimate quantitative factors? In the right context any quantitative measurement can be used as an essential success factor. Numerical growth? Sure. Place it in the context of the organizational purpose. For the church, it means reaching "unchurched" people. In any city there's a certain amount of rotation when it comes to the Christian community. Just moving those people from one church to the next is not necessarily an indicator of healthy growth. It's usually growth at the expense of the other churches. But, an assessment of the type of growth experienced could indicate that the church is fulfilling its mission. For instance, are we reconnecting "long-term out-of-church" people with our fellowship? Are we baptizing "new converts"? Numerical growth could also indicate we're fulfilling our discipleship responsibility, which includes disciples making disciples. Small group replication is another means of assessing the healthiness of the organization.

What about the financial side of it? To be sure, there has to be a certain level of capitalization that must be in place or the organization will cease to exist. Churches don't look at the same indicators as business, such as the PE ratio – price to earnings ratio. But, we can evaluate our

> *Make quantitative goals a part of the process, not the end point.*

stewardship emphasis and giving trends per capita. Are they above or below national averages or even denominational averages? Be cautious in using these standards, since every church has its own unique demographic. While profit doesn't drive us, we do have to be concerned about revenue and expenses, just like any business. The reality is that for an organization to grow it has to have the financial resources necessary for personnel, facilities management, and program development.

Branding is a common marketing term for creating a unique identity or product recognition, and yes, for churches and not-for-profit groups, the identity and reputation in the community is critical.

Quantitative Conclusions: Make quantitative goals a part of the process, not the end point. The best way of keeping this in perspective is by looking at the trends in the areas that you've identified. If your review incorporates trends, then you're focusing on process and continuous improvements - not terminal results. Trends may give you a picture of how well your core values pervade your organization, and ultimately it's healthy to gauge how well those values have been adopted by employees, volunteers, members, and participants.

Take Away Realities

- In Christian circles, we have too often allowed success to be determined by the raw data of attendance; we may feel less than successful if the data doesn't support a growth trend.
- The baseline, or plumb line, for determining success is related to faithfulness to our call and purpose. Success may be defined as "doing faithfully what you are called to do."
- There are qualitative factors in gauging success, such as: understanding and fulfilling your call, maintaining your character, and creating a healthy organizational culture.
- Some of the qualitative factors are relative to the individual – goals that you set that are unique to you.
- When balanced by qualitative criteria, and undergirded by faithfulness to your call, quantitative data can be helpful as benchmarks toward the larger purpose.
- Don't confuse benchmarks with the end goal; quantitative goals are just a part of the process, and they may help you understand how well the core values of your organization have been adopted.
- Carefully decide which quantitative factors are worthy of review and will provide an accurate picture of where the organization stands.

Core Questions for Success Re-Defined

1. Identify someone you consider to be a successful leader and then ask the questions: Why do I think they are successful? What gauge am I applying to my estimation of their success?

2. How could the following statement be true: being a leadership star is an emotionally dangerous place to be?

3. Do you agree with the assertion, and why or why not: size does not automatically equal success.

4. The baseline presented in this chapter for gauging success is faithfulness. Review your calling and consider how effectively you are fulfilling that calling. Answer the question: Am I faithfully doing what I know to do? Explain why do I believe this?

5. If you have not developed a personal mission statement, take time now to begin drafting an initial paragraph using the following criteria:
    a. keep it short, no more than two sentences, preferably one compact sentence
    b. use specific terminology, not generic or ambiguous
    c. apply it to one area, for example, your leadership role or professional calling
    d. revisit the statement frequently to verify its legitimacy

6. Based on the discussion of qualitative success, grade yourself concerning personal integrity and character – use a scale of 1 – 10 with ten being the greatest.

Are you building into your life a process that develops, or conversely, diminishes character? Explain your answer.

7. List and discuss with a close friend several of your personal goals. Are they realistic, reachable, and relevant to your life?

8. What appropriate quantitative benchmarks have you developed? List them and reflect on their validity.

Core Cases for Success Re-Defined

Case Study 1: A pastor and his church have been named *Church and Pastor of the Year* by their state convention - leading the state in growth percentages, baptisms, and contributions to the national denominational programs. But as the next year begins the pastor is exhausted, stretched thin, and easily irritated in conversations. He is pushing his staff to continue or exceed last year's trend. There is tension in the weekly staff meetings, and the other ministers feel that the pastor is being unrealistic in his expectations.

    a. Has this pastor fallen into the success trap?

    b. In what ways might the pastor re-adjust his understanding of success to reflect the presentation of this chapter?

Case Study 2: In a small town that is slowly dying, the Community Church of Anywhere is also seeing decreased attendance. The outreach programs are consistent, the worship is dynamic, the preaching is solid, and the ministries are healthy. The people genuinely seem to care for each other and there is little or no dissension. Everything is good, but the church is not growing numerically and while its influence is still very positive in the community, the congregation is reflecting an older demographic.

    a. How would you feel if you were the pastor?

    b. What assessment would you give the church: successful, unsuccessful, and why?

Case Study 3: In a rapidly growing city of approximately 75,000 people, there are many great churches of various denominations. Three or four of the churches have boomed to the point they have become mega churches exceeding 3,000 in attendance each Sunday. You, however, are the pastor of a medium-sized church running approximately 400 each Sunday. The competition is quite stiff and the larger churches seem to have momentum; subsequently the prospect pool is consistently feeding the mega churches to the detriment of your church's growth. You've tried everything you know to do, and all your efforts have yielded little numerical growth. As you look at your congregation and church ministries, there are no glaring problems.

    a.   Do you feel successful or unsuccessful?

    b.   How might you apply the presentation of this chapter to your circumstance?

SECTION TWO

___

Initiating Leadership

"If you don't lead, someone will,
and it may go where you don't want it to."

CHAPTER 5

Forfeited Leadership

"If you don't lead, someone will, and it (the organization) may go where you don't want it to." The truth of that statement is self-evident. Every organization needs a leader, and someone will eventually rise to the occasion. Yet, there's little guarantee that the organization or church will get to where it should under the tutelage of a de facto leader who assumes the reins. Let's suppose that you've been called to lead organization "x", and let's assume in that organization there are competing visions for direction with people vying for control. Sound familiar? If you don't provide the kind of leadership that is respected or fully assume your positional role as leader, someone will fill the gap. Forfeit means *to give up rights to* or *turn over control* to someone else, which is precisely what happens when the leader, by inaction or disqualification, loses that effectiveness.

Leaders must be proactive not reactive, and the twins, inaction and indecision, shut down the process of leadership. Inaction occurs when we do not nurture or persist in moving forward the vital systems of the organization. Inaction happens when a leader assumes an idle posture or shifts into neutral and doesn't address the critical issues at hand. There's a time for retreat and rebuilding reserves, but inaction is like the crack in the dam that allows water to force a failure in the structure. A proactive leader is patient and willing to wait on the development of a process, but he has laid the groundwork for the successful resolution of an issue. He sets in motion the systems that will build from latency to potency in a reasonable amount of time.

Inaction transpires when we either don't pay attention to the details of an organization's health, or in other cases when the leader withdraws from interacting in important decisions. Presence and participation in the system process of your church is critical. Withdrawing from interactions with staff or teams, a form of leadership monasticism, creates a gap or vacuum that will be filled by someone else. It could result in a shut down of the organizational activity. For example, the coach on the sideline is intrinsically involved in the play action on the field, not as a spectator but as one who makes important decisions that influence the game. The role of coach is far removed from that of spectator, but the leader who refuses interaction with key players or neglects to guide them through directional shifts, is just like the spectator in the stands.

Conversely, assuming responsibility and acting as a healthy and reliable leader stabilizes your organization. It brings a calmness and fortitude to the uncertainty of the "next steps." Active leadership doesn't have to be domineering to be

> *Active leadership doesn't have to be domineering to be effective, it just has to be deliberate and intentional.*

effective; it just has to be deliberate and intentional. This creates in people the comprehension that you are the leader, and that there is a future ahead of them.

I remember a weekend conference for a previous church where a group discussed directions and strategies. I concluded by saying, "I'll point the way, if you will go with me there." It was both an affirmation of my desire to actively engage in leadership, and an invitation for the other church leaders to go with me. It was a successful launch in a new direction.

Inaction is fed by indecision. It cripples and forfeits your leadership; it shows you're unwilling to assume the responsibility. In these terms, I'm not talking about taking the time to carefully weigh the pros and cons, the impact of a direction on your organization, or to give appropriate time for clarity. Sometimes waiting is appropriate. But, when the crucible is pressing, the crisis is impending, the work has slowed, and the show has stopped because of you, that is indecision. At those moments you lose your leadership.

I've noticed a couple of things that drive indecision: fear and over-analysis. Fear is a baseline emotion, God given for the purpose of safeguarding foolish acts or harmful behaviors. But fear, when it becomes a governing force in one's life, can be debilitating, or even ironically, a powerful motivator to act in a way hurtful to others. In the organizational dynamic of leadership, fear-motivated self-preservation leads to either indecision or to power plays and manipulation to perpetuate one's role. All are unhealthy.

Fear of reprisal can lead to indecision. Leaders are easy targets and sometimes suffer greatly when leading an organization to risk change or to challenge the status quo. There is often a "price to pay" when making decisions. If the leader hasn't developed the ability to weather the storm, the onslaught, itself, can cause the leader to return to the dock. I've made a number of decisions that I intuitively knew would bring reprisal or create difficulties for me. Yet, with certainty of the direction and confidence in the process that I had walked through, I was willing to walk forward and "tough it out" for the duration.

What about the threat and tyranny of the collective "they"? Long known and discussed in pastor's groups and leadership circles, the power of the collective "they" must be evaluated. How many are "they?" What influence do "they" really have in the organization? What are the motivations "they" have? When someone uses the plural "they" it's sometimes a cover for "we," or at the least, an undisclosed number who like the *Heterodon* (commonly called a puff adder, or the American hog-nosed snake) likes to appear larger, cobra-like, and more menacing than it really is. In particular this adder, if unsuccessful in scaring its predator, will often roll on its back as though dead. What a vivid picture of the manner in which "they" attempt to bluff and bully, but in reality often are less capable of intimidation.

Over the years, I've developed a few observations about "they." Frequently, the collective group is much smaller than intimated by the bearer of the message. The use of "they" is almost certainly an attempt to maximize the pressure and influence of the outside group. The reticence of the emissary to divulge members of the collective is not normally for the protection of the people, but a desire to not expose the limited number of persons involved. In addition, "they" typically project their own feelings onto the perspective of others and assume that they have larger support than they actually do. It's a perspective based on a monocular view point and they believe others agree with them, and in essence see it their way, when in reality they may not.

Which leads to the second observation: there is usually a point person or a small cluster of individuals who are the most intense and lathered about the issue. Practically speaking, there are varying degrees of intensity among those who are enumerated in the collective "they." Some may be in partial agreement but not as strongly biased as the most radical of the collective. There are usually some firebrands who stir, agitate, and goad others to join in the movement, but not all have the same passion or desire for the proverbial "lynching." You may be able to diffuse some of the angst by reaching out to the secondary level instigators.

The third observation is that the emissary may be the ring leader, but in some cases, he or she is the one whom the collective "they" think may be the best received when conveying the bad news. In essence, it's an attempt to lend credibility to the complaint or issue, with the hope of leveraging the inside relationship to increase the poignancy of the problem.

I found myself in the middle of a movement on one occasion when I served as an associate in a church. I became the "go to" person, (eventually serving as the collective voice) and I shared with the individual the concerns of the collective. I remember distinctly presenting the information as an unbiased observer who just forwarded the message. But as that messenger, I unwittingly placed myself in the middle of the interpersonal conflict between others, and in retrospect I should have been more cautious. Significant unease and conflict developed subsequently and the church began to decline, not because of my actions, but as a result of the conflict. Now, many years later, I realize I could have removed myself completely from the issue and avoided some of the personal distress associated with the problem.

Even with the above comments, I hasten to add that the leader should evaluate carefully the breadth of the collective before making a sweeping generalization. If there are key leaders included in that group, you could face significant obstacles. I know there are times when the movement gains such force and longevity that the leader may not be able to survive (nor should he try to). A careful analysis of the scope of influence may yield a better determination of the seriousness of the assault.

Fear of harm to the organization, when the leader is most concerned about the welfare of the group, can lead to indecision. There may be some leaders who fear division or crisis so much that they are unwilling to address critical issues. They deny that there's a problem and diminish the seriousness of the crisis, or believe if ignored, that it will go away.

Fear of losing positional power may prompt some to become more isolationists in making decisions, but I've learned from experience that there's benefit in collaborative decision making. This requires confidence and certainty on the part of the leader, but is especially helpful for the team "buy in" since they feel they've been a part in the process. Collaborative discussion doesn't lessen your leadership, it enhances it. When one has the respect of others and the positional roles are clear, the process can be very healthy. I usually don't make decisions in isolation.

Another aspect of the positional power issue can lead to an organizational melt down. If the leader is operating from an emotional and leadership deficit, he may grasp too tightly or push too hard, resulting in over-controlling the organization. If fear drives you and your concern is losing organizational power, the consequences lead to forfeiting the organizational purpose. Eventually, the end result lessens your own leadership position; truly one of the authentic benchmarks is to ascertain how well our organization is fulfilling its purpose.

Another component that creates difficulty, overanalyzing, is a common malady resulting in indecision. My wife and I jokingly refer to this using the common phrase: paralysis of analysis. I don't know where this expression first found traction, but it's an accurate portrayal of how we sometimes grind to a halt. When stuck here, the best steps include securing wise counsel from another person to corroborate your thoughts and intentions, then on to an assessment of when the decision has to be made. Timing is a critical part of the process, and knowing when the "trigger" has to be pulled will eventually force a decision. A word of caution: when you gauge the process accurately, yet go past that moment in time, you have in effect made a decision and you release yourself to consequences that may be beyond your control.

I'm an instrument-rated private pilot, and timing is a key factor as a part of some instrument procedures. In particular, in one NDB (non-directional beacon) approach that I commonly practice, the clocking of three minutes and eight seconds is critical. At a certain marker I begin the timer, and when I reach the correct altitude followed by the correct passage of time, I either continue the approach to land or declare a missed approach and immediately begin the appropriate re-routing. I have a definitive point that is mission critical. We, too, must understand the dynamics of our situation and recognize when those moments come and go. Inaction at the moment of crisis ultimately results in a default decision and is virtually never healthy. The motto, "do something, even if it's wrong" is a hardly the best advice, but when faced with a deadline you have to make the best decision with the best information you have at that moment. Don't look back!

The technique of artificial dead-lining: How do I normally work through the process of evaluating options? As I draw close to making a decision, I've already made a trial run on the choices and considered the possible consequences. To do this I set an artificial deadline, days or weeks in advance, of when an official decision has to be made. I'll say, "If I had to make the decision right now, which way would I go, which person would I choose, or what step would I take?" Using my comment above, *Make the best decision with the best information you have at the moment!* I force myself to decide, but with the understanding that I'm under no obligation to follow through on the momentary decision. It still gives me a way to look at, mull over, and think about how it might impact my organization in the days and weeks ahead. I recently asked my staff to help me

> Make the best decision with the best information you have at that moment.

make a decision; about a third of the way through the process I asked them, "If you had to decide today, right now, what would you choose?" I explained that this was a decision making exercise and I wouldn't hold them to it. They could change their minds at the next level. It was still uncomfortable and created a little anxiety, but it gave me an honest, gut impression of their thoughts. An artificial deadline can allow you to test the water, and at the least gauge your own reaction to a decision.

The Disqualified Leader: Forfeited leadership also arises from being disqualified in some way from the role in which you serve. For Christian leaders, the concept of disqualification is an all too familiar category that typically includes moral failures, disrupted relationships, burnout, or pressured terminations.

When an event or incident occurs that breaks faith with your organization, it's difficult to reclaim the respect and ability to lead. Even if you retain positional leadership, the personal side of the equation is shot. At the heart of all this is TRUST. There is no greater tool on the belt of the leader than building and maintaining trust. Trust is the money in the leadership bank and the currency for transactions of transition. It's the filter that allows people to believe the best when decisions are made. It's earned by consistent actions and through the developing of relationships. It's usually not given quickly, but it can be lost in an instant! On the level of decision making, the leader must consider the impact of his actions upon a wide range of people in the organization? If not, trust is diminished.

> *Trust is usually not given quickly, but it can be lost in an instant!*

87

Protect the trust relationship by building into your life safeguards, such as: accountability with peers, professional mentors who sharpen you, and friends who occasionally challenge you with truthful words and insight. Create a greater capacity to listen without defensiveness when a critique is given. Don't dismiss too quickly the criticism you hear second hand. Ask, is there something to learn here?

For over twenty years I've met monthly with a group of my peers. There have been times when I've made contributions into the lives of the other pastors or leaders, but certainly I have benefited more by listening to their comments and incorporating their reflections on the things I've shared. This isn't an accountability group, but it's often brought issues to the forefront that I need to consider. Many times, just noting their struggles helps me with mine.

In vocations where character is an essential element, a moral failure is one of the most damaging ways of breaking trust with your people. Dependent upon the type of problem, the leader may even be immediately relieved of his position and subsequently can only begin a path of restoration and probable relocation. The directing structure will normally decide the level of correction required for the errant leader, but the larger issue is the effect upon the members of your organization. If the leader is able to stay in place, then the process of repairing and rebuilding relationships must begin. There must be appropriate humility and repentance, a plan for re-instating the leader to his role, and time for the leader to re-establish healthy relationships with members. It takes much more time than when the leader first began his work. It will take a long-term demonstration of sensitivity, consistency, and moral safeguards!

If termination has occurred, the leader still can begin a process of restoration; especially, if there are issues that should be addressed through professional counseling or with a mentor who can carefully guide him through the process. Relocation or re-vocation is a necessity, but only after adequately dealing with the personal issues. A leader should not take his unresolved problems and parachute into the next place, as though there's nothing wrong or that a change of venue will solve the dilemma. It's probable that there will be trouble there, also.

Forfeiting leadership happens on many levels: by deferring to another person in the organization, by abdicating an active role in the decision making process, or even through a major misjudgment or moral failure. Successful leaders are those who know themselves and their personal weaknesses, and sufficiently safeguard against a debilitating misstep.

Take Away Realities

- If you don't lead, someone will, and it (the organization) may end up where you don't want it to.
- Carefully consider the breadth and impact of "they." "They" are often not as powerful as they seem.
- Indecision and Inaction are crippling characteristics of poor leaders. Work to overcome their debilitating effects, in part, by applying the following realities.
- Do not lead from a position of fear. If the leader fears losing organizational power, it often results in a forfeiture of the organizational purpose.
- Resist over-analyzing the components of a decision.
- Make the best decision with the best information you have at the moment!
- Set an artificial deadline to provide a test case for the decision.
- Abrupt disqualification may occur through moral failures, disrupted relationships, burnout, or pressured terminations.
- One of the greatest tools in leadership is trust. It isn't earned quickly, but can be lost in an instant.
- Protect your life and leadership by putting safeguards in place: such as appropriate accountability and authentic peer friendships that challenge you.

- Deal with issues through appropriate counsel and mentorship. Don't transport your issues to the next position.
- If necessary, walk through a process of restoration.

Mark W. Gregory

Core Questions for Leadership Forfeiture

1. If the statement is true: "if you don't lead, someone will, and it may go where you don't want it to," then how does that impact your organization if someone else took the reins and moved it in a different direction? Where is the end point of the other vision compared to your vision?

2. Are you currently abdicating your leadership responsibilities, and how might you reassert yourself into the process?

3. Of the two leadership maladies, inaction and indecision, which is your greater struggle? Using a concept from this chapter: Has the show stopped because of you? Why?

4. Consider the role of each member of your core leadership team, who is participating and who has withdrawn?

5. Discuss the ways that fear shuts down participation in the leadership process.

6. Identify a group or movement in your environment that reflects the collective "they." Ask the questions presented in this chapter: How many are they? What influence do they really have? Who is their point person, and what is his role in the complaint? Does everyone in the opposing group have the same intensity level? If you challenge and confront the issue, can you survive the crisis?

7. Provide an honest assessment of your positional authority. Are your decisions impacted by the fear of losing that authority?

8. Consider the technique of an artificial deadline and apply that to a pending decision. If you had to make the decision "right now" which way would you lean and what impact might that have on the organization?

9. Are you facing issues that could disqualify you from serving? How have you built trust or how have you lost trust?

10. Consider who and why you might consider a mentor to help you through this difficulty.

11. Is there a need for the process of restoration in your life? List the personal steps that would produce healthy result.

12. Are there safeguards in your life that protect you from disqualification? If you were to begin a peer or accountability group, what would it look like, and who might you include?

Core Cases for Leadership Forfeiture

Case Study 1: The Pastor of Crossbridge Community Church has led the church for seven years. Significant growth has occurred, but the multiple changes and transitions have taken a toll on his leadership. He feels battled and worn, and his staff has noticed that he is spending more time in his office, cuts the staff meetings short, and refrains from giving them input on their ministries. There is very little strategic planning, and not only has the church hit a plateau, but there's a general level of malaise in the programming. The chairman of a powerful committee has assumed a greater role in making decisions that affect the vision and direction of the church, and subsequently the trend of the programming is reversing the changes of the last several years. The staff has met with the pastor and asked him what he's going to do about it – but so far he's not provided a plan for forward movement.

> a. Describe the paralysis of the pastor using the concepts of this chapter: inaction, indecision, paralysis.
> b. Has he abdicated his leadership? What personal strategies might he implement to regain his ability to lead?

Case Study 2: After years of faithful service, the leader of a local social ministry has crashed and burned. He hasn't experienced a moral failure, but has betrayed the trust of his members with frequent caustic outbursts and by making rash decisions without regard for employees or the impact upon the organization. Both are unusual and very out-of-character for him. Because of the alienation and high level of tension, the board has stepped in and conducted several intervention meetings, hoping to curb the antagonism. They have most recently given him a two week leave of absence to rethink his actions and consider his long-term relationship with the organization. They will then reconvene with him and decide his fate based on his attitude and posture at that time.

    a. What steps might this leader take that would deal with both personal and organizational issues?

    b. What benefits could a long-term mentor or peer group provide for this leader?

    c. Describe a possible process of restoration that would allow this leader to maintain his position, or that would assist him as he begins work in another organization.

CHAPTER 6

Leadership Models: The Balance of the Fulcrum
& Styles versus Skills

What's your profile, temperament, level of assertiveness? What's your style? How do you classify yourself as a leader? There are a multitude of models that assess leadership styles and propose compatibility with different types of organizations. Most are based on characteristics such as personality preferences and vocational statistics. They often categorize people and project the likelihood of success in certain fields. Yet, like you, I've seen unlikely leaders ride the crest of huge swells, and I've seen assertive leaders flounder on the shoals, pounded time and time again, unable to make it past the first breakers.

Can we agree on this: there is no "one style" of leadership that can be predictive of a successful follower-ship. Since leadership styles don't always equal leadership skills, how can we reduce (there's that concept again: reduce or strip it all away) the discussion to some basic realities?

I prefer to simplify by using two terms: *demonstrative* and *communicative*, and thereby develop a balance of these two as an effective means of leading into an organizational growth cycle. There is no need to eliminate one or the other, for both are needed, valued, and weighted at different times and in distinct ways. But we, through the shaping of our personalities and skills, tend to default to one or the other of these. Even though the occasional swing is normal, a total default to one leads to ineffectual leadership. In some sense, all leadership is communicated, so my classifications may seem somewhat stilted; to distinguish between the two modes, we'll refer to the demonstrative mode as "do what I do" and the communicative mode as "do what I say."

Demonstrative Leadership: Do what I do.

The concept of servant leadership is well known, and in its basic form, constitutes a means of leading others by serving them. Demonstrative leadership is slightly different in that it's primarily a modeling skill, incorporating serving to create independent action. We teach and lead by example; we show others what we want done and then expect them to do it. We become coaches who first roll on the ground before looking up and saying, that's how it's done.

On a mission trip to Honduras in 1999, I found myself in the second phase of the trip as a foreman designing a weight bearing-beam for a construction project. My dad was a part of the mission team, and as we drew to the close of our time, he asked, "How do you know how to do this?" I was dumbfounded by the question, since I thought the answer was self-evident. "Daddy, I learned it from you." The power of demonstrative leadership is in part its ability to be caught or imitated by others. We show it,

> *The power of demonstrative leadership is its ability to be caught or imitated by others.*

they do it. It can be natural transference of healthy behavior and organizational process. Let's be aware of how quickly our employees and volunteers see and integrate our actions into their own lives in a trickle down manner.

Demonstrative leadership *portrays* the commonality of the vision. Critical to the success of a vision is the perception that the leader and other participants are all in this thing together. An ivory tower leader will quickly lose the in-the-trench followers. Top-heavy orders without full participation by the leader lends to exasperation on the part of the workers. Followers want and need to see that the leader is with them on the journey. It reinforces that the leader, too, believes in the vision enough to join them in the work. Unquestionably, the presence of the leader contributes to perseverance on the part of followers. I've found that my presence and participation at an event builds camaraderie, respect, and a positive perception of leadership.

We also like to think that no one is above the law … similarly, we like to think that no one is above the work. We cannot afford to create an appearance that we're above certain types of work, however menial the job may seem to be. I love it when I answer the phone at the office and identify myself; people often say, "I didn't expect to get you" as though implying that the pastor shouldn't answer the phone. Why not? If there's a gap, I should fill it. Each week we move chairs in our sanctuary, and whenever possible after the service, I grab chairs and start arranging them in stacks just like everybody else. The last thing a leader needs is the mentality: I'm too important, indispensable, or too good to do that! If that's our attitude, what does that say about how we value our employees?

This type of leadership reinvigorates the troops, and helps affirm that what others are doing, large or small, is important. It gives the leader a unique opportunity to encourage and express appreciation for the things that others do.

I also sense that this mode of leading is helpful in re-envisioning the future and refocusing the place of change. It allows the leader to course-correct along the way by keeping in close touch with those who are following. Never a bad idea! Subtle shifts may present themselves as the organization grows and changes. If the leader is far removed from the field of operation, then he or she may lose the capability of seeing a better way across the battle field.

Demonstrative leadership is very effective, but is limited in that as the organization grows, it loses it's effectiveness, not by virtue of setting an example but by the inability to be in multiple places at all times. Despite our intentions or our occasional self deceptions, we are not omnipresent.

It's also time intensive, and at some point there has to be an honest assessment of one's time and how it's best spent. This acknowledgement leads to the second of the classifications, which balances out the palate of the leader's skills: communicative leadership.

Communicative Leadership: Do what I say.

Larger or more complex organizations still require demonstrative leadership but lean more heavily on communicative leadership. Remember the statement: Do what I say. This is the essence of communicative leadership.

Communicative leadership is more directive, but must be backed up by the respect that a leader engenders. We've long heard of positional authority and personal authority; in this case, personal authority carries the day. Yes, I know that positional authority is a necessity in organizations and it does give a leader some leverage, especially in a for-profit corporation where remuneration is tied to performance. But in reality, if people meet the letter of the law, they're more concerned about doing only what they have to do, not what needs to be done for the benefit of the organization. So, the baseline of a communicative leader is derived from his or her ability to translate their own personal authority into action on the part of followers. Remember the definition of a committed follower: those who *know the vision*, **trust the leader**, and whose *personal spiritual journey aligns with the long-term goal of the organization*. To reiterate: trust and respect for the leader are necessary.

For communicative leadership to be effective, the leader must speak clearly of the vision, the goals, and the strategy that gets the journey done. Followers are not blind (nor do they often follow blindly), but they generally respond to a well articulated vision. What tools in the box help a leader communicate clearly? Images, verbal portraits, defining the end goal, succinct statements that drive home a poignant point, all of these are means of punctuating the vision. I'm of the mind that long vision statements are destined to fade and fail. Who can remember them much less understand their greater scope? If it's over two lines, it's too long. And if the leader has to expound on the vision statement, he's already losing ground.

Clarity also comes by spelling out expectations for both individuals as well as setting benchmarks for the organization. While we can't predict the future, we can set attainable goals that can be celebrated and which become the launch pad for the next part of the journey. Resetting the goal line is one way of drawing people further on the journey.

A huge part of communicative leadership is repetitive effort. From first-hand experience, I can verify that people seldom get the full scope of the vision in the first go around. It has to be said over, and over, and over. You get it! Make it loud! Grab their attention. Be creative.

Styles versus Skills?

I'll repeatedly affirm that a variety of styles can effectively lead an organization, yet, we do need to differentiate between styles and skills. A particular style is more likely a part of your DNA and personality make up, but skills can be learned and developed! While some leaders are stronger in some skills than others, everyone can show improvement in the basic skills of leadership. And they are ...?

Relational skill is at the top of the list, and is an area where there is little excuse for failure from the leader. Abrasive, abrupt, aggressive, harsh, and mean-spirited behaviors have no place in the

> *The greatest leverage comes from relationships that are forged, not forced, and cultivated, not coerced.*

relational attributes of the Christian leader; I would contend this is true for any leader in any organization. I've consistently heard people excuse bad behavior by shrugging it off as a personality quirk, or otherwise justifying it as an only response to a particular set of circumstances. Relational strength derives from the ability to cultivate appropriate friendships, alliances, and professional associations that allow people to be a part of your leadership world. The greatest leverage comes from relationships that are forged, not forced, and cultivated, not coerced. Our goal in leadership is to invite our employees and volunteers to engage in the larger organization dynamic and thus willingly contribute to the process of growth.

Relational skills also allow you to navigate change much more smoothly, especially when people know that you are sensitive to their needs and aware of the pain that is caused by organizational transition. When people know you care about them and the strength of your friendship guides you in seeing more clearly their perspective, they are more apt to walk with you. Another particular correlation for building better relationship skills is the pleasure and friendship that comes from mutually attaining a goal. What is a celebration if you don't have someone to celebrate it with?

Multitasking is another skill that can be developed. I've just about decided that time management is a myth or an urban legend over which even the most disciplined person has difficulty gaining control. At best it is elusive, at worst, it is impossible. For me, it's better to think in terms of imminent tasks that require daily attention (I list them and get them done in the most expedient fashion), and longer term priorities. I recognize that I will accomplish those things that are important to me and fit into the larger framework of my life and ministry.

A different approach is to consider how to nurture several projects at once, which requires some advance planning. One rule of thumb is to give yourself enough time to work them through the process without killing yourself along the way. Some things are time critical and some aren't. Discerning the difference helps you pace yourself and relieve some of the pressure. Another suggestion is to develop a method that keeps the project in front of you, such as a flow chart, spreadsheet, or calendar tickler reminders that you set for each week. I'm a visual person, so anything I can do to regularly bring it into view is a good thing.

Tipping the scales ...

So what about the balance of styles? We definitely tend to gravitate to one side or the other: demonstrative or communicative. I fall clearly into the demonstrative camp. I'm always right in the middle of everything, with a shovel, hammer, or vacuum. It's my default mode – almost to the point that I succumb to the thought that a job can't be done without me. What I've discerned, however, after honestly assessing my own style, is that I do often work out of the communicative mode.

A balance of these two is the healthiest place to be for a leader, but note that a balance doesn't have to be perfect equilibrium. It can be weighted slightly more to one side and occasionally even fluctuate back and forth. Actually, as an organization grows and changes, the leader must be willing to change also. By necessity, a larger more complex organization will require more communicative leadership. This shift frequently doesn't occur naturally for the leader, and some find themselves no longer able to function in the culture of that organization. But, the good news is that most leaders can adjust to the adaptations of the corporate culture and extend their usefulness as leaders.

Take Away Realities

- There are many styles of leadership and no one style is predictive of success.
- An easy way to categorize our leadership mode of operation is to think in terms of demonstrative leadership or communicative leadership. Demonstrative leadership can be summarized as "Do what I do," and communicative leadership as "Do what I say."
- The power of demonstrative leadership is its ability to be caught or imitated by others.
- The baseline of a communicative leader is derived from his or her ability to translate their own personal authority into action by the followers.
- The greatest leverage comes from relationships that are forged, not forced, and cultivated, not coerced.

Core Questions for Leadership Models

1. Have you felt restricted in your leadership by a narrow definition of your leadership style, and whether your style is "typically" successful in your field? Do you agree or disagree with the statement: there is no one style of leadership that can be predictive of a successful followership? Why?

2. After having studied the concepts of demonstrative leadership and communicative leadership, which of the two is your default mode of operation? Does this surprise you and why? Describe an example that highlights your default mode.

3. Why might the demonstrative leadership model have a greater capacity for emulation? Note the statement: The power of demonstrative leadership is its ability to be caught or imitated by others. Do you agree, and why?

4. Is there a closer connection of leader and followers with demonstrative leadership than communicative leadership? If so, what are some of the natural results of this close correlation?

5. Give an example of a leader where you've seen the following self-perception, and what was your opinion of that leader. The last thing a leader needs is the mentality: I'm too important, indispensable, or too good to do that!

6. List and describe some of the advantages and disadvantages of the demonstrative style of leadership?

7. Communicative leadership is best summarized by the statement: Do what I say. How do the concepts of positional and personal authority correlate to the communicative style?

8. In your estimation, how does the building of trust between leader and followers add to the communicative style?

9. List the tools in the box that produce a well articulated vision. Add to the short list in this chapter.

10. How does relational skill bring leverage to the process of leadership? Do you agree that the "greatest leverage comes from relationships that are forged, not forced; cultivated nor coerced?" Identify areas of personal weakness and describe strategies that help you develop strengths.

11. Consider how well you balance the demonstrative and communicative styles.

Core Cases for Leadership Models

Case Study 1: A young leader has studied the personality and approach of a high profile and apparently successful leader, with a view to emulate his leadership style and traits. He had the opportunity to meet the leader at a conference and scheduled an appointment for the next day before it concluded. After meeting for coffee between the two morning sessions, he thanked the leader and took his notes to an outside patio to reflect on what he had learned. First, the leader's personality was more reserved, not the outgoing charismatic persona he had expected. Second, he predicted the leader to have strong management skills, but it seemed that the opposite was true, since much of the administration was left to others on his staff. And last, the leader advised him to spend more time on developing his own leadership style, rather than copying others. All of these observations left him disconcerted, since he was looking for someone to model his own leadership after. He left the conference more puzzled than ever.

> a. How had the young man made an error in attempting to emulate the behavior of the older leader?
> b. What assumptions did the young man bring to the conversation about leadership?
> c. If you were to counsel this young leader, what would you tell him to do next?

Case Study 2: A chief executive in a fast growing company is struggling with personal leadership transitions. The organization started small, and he was able to keep his hands involved in virtually every decision and directional change. Now, the number of employees has tripled, multiple departments have been put in place to cover various operations of the business, the sales force has moved the company from regional to national. The executive is feeling overwhelmed and ill-equipped to handle the organizational changes, much less to rethink his own mode of operation. He has taken a few days off to get a grip on how he best needs to lead the company. He's reflecting on the concepts that he's just read concerning demonstrative leadership and communicative leadership, and it's clear that his default mode has been demonstrative. His strengths include a high relational capability - several of the employees are his closest friends - but he is weak in the area of multitasking, and conceptualizing the organizational structure.

> a. In the context of this chapter, how might the leader accept the positive aspects of his default mode? What steps might he then take to develop the communicative leadership role that the organization requires. How can he balance the two?
>
> b. How important is his relational strength in leading the organization? In your estimation, does this hinder or optimize his leadership? In what ways?
>
> c. As presented in the case study, he is weaker in the area of multitasking, so what steps might

he take to produce healthy systems that result in better management?

CHAPTER 7

Traits That Command Attention

In the subsets of styles and skills, there are underlying traits that surface in leaders who have successfully journeyed with a group of people. These characteristics are like balustrades that bolster rail structures or floor joists that span and support the project above. They are necessary components in the process of leadership even though they are below the surface. Noticeable only when the observer looks behind the scenes and studies the flow of leadership, they appear effortless and natural but in reality may have been birthed in stressful moments of personal discovery and learning.

While the list of traits could be lengthy, and rightfully so, there are four that bear deeper examination: *passion, humility, intuition,* and *creativity.* Obvious commodities for leadership, passion and creativity are frequently associated with successful leadership, and ironically, humility and intuition are not. Humility is considered a virtue of moral behavior and incorrectly conjures images of meekness, passivity and acquiescence, traits not normally valued in the boardroom. Intuition is the perceived guesswork or artsy side of leadership, hard to objectify and categorize, but whose results are tangible. In these pages I present a case for the inclusion of these two oddballs.

Are these traits inherent in certain people and not in others? I don't think so. Everyone has some portion of these traits, though in varying degrees. I believe that most people can develop passion, especially when their lives become centered on a purpose that solidifies the expenditure of their resources: primarily financial and temporal. Humility is a relational posture and may be the hardest of the four to command; it can't be falsified – pseudo humility is "no humility." It has to be developed through difficult life lessons and a growing respect for our place in relationship with others, and with our Lord. Intuition is an early developmental trait that we each have, but sometimes we diminish its force as we learn other means of relating to the world and others around us. Likewise, creativity which is easily noted in children (with imaginary friends and spontaneous play acting) loses its power in our lives as we attempt to fit into a more structured learning environment. Let's reclaim, relearn, and replenish these traits.

The Power of Passion ...

Passion infuses the leadership style of the individual with the critical elements of enticement and endurance; truly few people will follow a leader who is passionless. Why follow someone who doesn't believe in "what he's selling?" In most successful organizations there is usually a passionate leader even if that person is not the positional leader. What typically occurs is that the one who has passion will rise to a leadership level and sometimes supplant the "official" leader. What makes this trait so compelling and how do we recognize it?

You think you would know it when you see it, but it's not as easily identified. Passion is an intriguing concept: it's an internal conviction infused with outward focus, energy, personal investment, possibly even extreme sacrifice. It could be confused with enthusiasm, but this is an inadequate gauge. If we observed someone at an amusement park step off the roller coaster and immediately get back in line, we probably wouldn't generally call that passion. We'd call it an adrenaline rush or extreme excitement, maybe enthusiasm, but not passion. Contrast that with the same amusement experience, but as I saw recently on a cable channel, of a group with a determined agenda to ride all the top coasters in the nation. They strategically planned their vacations and routes to meet certain goals and deadlines. They were driven. I'd call that passion.

We might also confuse passion with emotion. To be sure, the passionate person has a great deal of investment in the object of the passion, but emotions range through a wide spectrum and may be deceptive regarding the longevity of a particular pursuit. Passion is a clear representation of a person's strong urgency to obtain, accomplish or fulfill a desire, dream, or vision. As a quality, passion is the next level up from enthusiasm or mere

> *Passion is a clear representation of a person's strong urgency to obtain, accomplish or fulfill a desire, dream, or vision.*

emotional response. It is more aptly described as the coalescing of a personal goal with the exhaustive effort it takes to achieve it.

As such, people tend to gather or congregate around common goals, and this is one reason that a passionate leader often has passionate followers. There's no doubt, either, that passion can be transferred and caught by others. It systemically seeps throughout an organization like water that soaks into wood. It is attractive; it garners the interest of others who have yet to develop their own passions, but who readily adopt the passion of others.

For an interest or goal to reach the level of a "passionate" pursuit, it must have a possessive quality. You have to own it yourself. It possesses you, drives you and becomes the center hub around which other things spin. It is the gravity field that keeps the "stuff" of your life from spinning out of control from centrifugal forces. There is, however, a difference between passion and obsession. The first is a healthy expression of values, goals, and commitments that establish precedents and patterns in life. The latter, obsession, occurs when an individual loses perspective and is controlled by the object of obsession, rather than setting normal and healthy boundaries.

Sometimes, we have to step back or get another's opinion to provide a realistic reflection of our passion. For something to be defined as a passion it has to be a persistent pursuit where one maintains focus even with considerable distractions and detours. A passing passion doesn't qualify and is more typical of a casual interest.

Simply ask: does the object of your passion have longevity in your life?

Genuine passion is costly. It becomes an expense of yourself, and takes a "pound of your flesh." It may even include suffering. The Encarta dictionary, as well as the popular movie, *The Passion,* depicts passion as the "sufferings" of Jesus. This is a clear indication that even in our secular society, the pursuit of our passion is understood as a costly venture. To achieve the object of passion, there are many who have been willing to sacrifice even their own lives. The famed evangelist of the 1700's, George Whitefield, is said to have exhausted his voice and physical frame from lifelong efforts of preaching in Great Britain and the American colonies. After one round of preaching in Scotland, he developed a respiratory ailment that never subsided. He often vomited blood after speaking to large crowds which necessitated straining his voice. The strenuous nature of his ministry and his infirmity certainly caused a premature death in his fifties. It's not as likely that we will suffer the same fate, but yet even today, there are many who consistently suffer for their faith – as often chronicled in a publication called *The Voice of the Martyrs.*

Most of us who are leaders will concede that there's an economy to the process of leadership. If economics can be understood as the system of cost that one uses to obtain goods or sustain a lifestyle, then we have significantly paid to "get there" as leaders. The negative side is frequently the expense to families and marriages. That's not always the necessary price, but it's "gonna" come out somewhere. Long before leaders experience the benefit of their labor, they work long hours, take personal hits, make difficult decisions, promote seasons of needed change, reshuffle the personnel rosters, and experience abandonment by those who have pledged to make the journey. It's a heavy toll. But the leader who understands the price tag on the front end and believes the journey is worth it, is the one who emerges as the leader at the end. Using my introduction analogy, he is the one standing at the helm of the ship when it arrives at port.

Take Away Realities

- While we've looked at the two larger categories of demonstrative and communicative styles of leadership, there are certainly a number of identifiable traits that enhance a leader's role. Among them are passion, humility, creativity, and intuition.
- Passion is an internal conviction infused with outward focus, energy, and personal investment. It's not to be confused with enthusiasm which may be temporary.
- As a quality, passion is the next level up from enthusiasm or mere emotional response. It is more aptly described as the coalescing of a personal goal with the exhaustive effort it takes to achieve it. Passion and obsession, however, are not the same.
- Passion can be "caught" by others.
- Genuine Passion is costly, with both a positive result and a potentially negative side.

Core Questions for Passion

1. Before reading this chapter, how might you have defined passion? Now what changes in perception do you have concerning the deeper nature of passion as compared to emotion or enthusiasm?
2. Are you willing to follow a leader who lacks passion? Why or why not?
3. How does the passion you observe in someone else motivate you?
4. List the interests or goals that you consider to be passions in your life.
5. Identify the items on your list that have longevity in your life. Does the list surprise you, and what would you drop off the list as not equaling the definition of a passion?
6. Describe which items on the list have proven costly and why. Consider the positive benefits of your passionate pursuits and then reflect on the negative.

A Core Case for Passion

Joseph is the new administrator of the local Homeless Help Ministry. He served on the Advisory Board for four years, and when the position became available, he applied for and was awarded the role. He has just completed his first monthly council meeting and has come to the realization that he doesn't have the passion to move the organization forward, or the leadership skills to make needed decisions. Not knowing of his lack of passion, the board has given him support and encouragement, telling him to take the time over the next couple of months to begin developing a longer term strategy and vision for the Ministry. He's confronted, however, with a dilemma: he needs the job, but he doesn't have a sincere interest in the organization. In fact, he had previously planned to resign from the board for lack of attentiveness to the mission of the group. When the job came open, he removed himself from the board with the thought that he would apply for the job. When he received the offer, he believed he could develop a stronger interest in the purpose of the organization, but the opposite has occurred. He's decided to stay and give the job his best effort, with the hopes that he'll rise to the occasion.

      a. What difference do you believe it would make if the leader was fully committed to the vision of the organization and had a genuine passion for it?

      b. Can he develop a passion for the work of the group, or is he incapable of personal growth in this area? What could he do to develop a greater interest?

c. Should he share with the board his dilemma, or sit on it until he can make a personal decision?

CHAPTER 8

The Power of Humility ...

Another admirable trait that seems in short supply in "high powered" executives and leaders is humility. I agree with Jim Collins in "Good to Great" that the Level 5 leaders (his highest level for a leader) have a unique combination of humility and will. These leaders build long lasting companies with lengthy return trends. In my estimation, humility is no new leadership commodity, but is richly heralded even as our Old Testament Scriptures speak negatively about the contrasting traits, which are the haughty eyes of the proud and the arrogance of the wealthy. Moses received the designation of meekness, and in the powerful hymn of Philippians chapter two, Christ demonstrated humility to the greatest degree possible – pouring himself out and taking the form of a servant.

What does the Bible teach about humility and its twin, meekness? Its very nature is power under control, strength under submission, and pride subjected to restraint. None of these phrases denote a weak persona. They profoundly depict significant influence and authority that refuses to take advantage of others or to show arrogance. Authentic humility becomes a pleasant personal attribute, and like passion, attracts people. It may not be as easily observed, it is sometimes misunderstood as weakness, and it is consistently discounted by the assertive leaders of the world. But there is a compelling bond that develops between the follower and the humble leader when humility is an ingredient of the relationship.

Genuine humility is not just that a person is self-effacing, and thereby consistently denigrating themselves or downplaying their role in the organization's success. These are false attestations that may still mask pride under the surface. Humility is an acceptance of the importance of others in our lives, the knowledge of where I fit into the fellowship and family of God, and the willingness to understand ministry as being under the direction of the Lord's authority.

Let's unpack that last statement: Humility is first an acknowledgement that we need others in our lives. Pride and arrogance lead us to say, "I don't need you" or "I can do this on my own." Conversely, humility as a trait affirms, "I do need you." It is an admission that "I can't do this alone." Humility triggers receptivity to other's input in the process of leadership and cultivates an open dialogue. The person who walks in humility allows others to invest in their lives, in essence, he or she learns to be a "receiver" and hear the truth that others speak. Clearly, a mark of humility is a teachable spirit. When hiring new employees, one of the traits I look for is the ability to receive instruction and respond to suggestions without defensiveness. This alerts me to their capacity to be teachable and open to shaping their skills.

> *One mark of humility is a teachable spirit.*

This thought leads me to question: how teachable am I? If I want to sharpen my own skills I have to be willing to allow someone to invest in my learning curve. Before my fiction novel, *Net Trigger*, was published in 2009, I shared a rough draft with a friend who is a well-known and accomplished author. She and her husband had been friends of ours since college. She returned the manuscript to me after conducting a thorough edit of the first chapter, with the comment, "I hope you'll still be my friend." She gave me an honest assessment with constructive comments on the technicalities of writing fiction. It was significantly helpful in refining my creative abilities (still in the honing stages). I could have been insulted, offended, or have simply disregarded her comments, but my posture was more teachable and I hope, more humble.

I genuinely wanted the feedback that would make me a better writer. By the time this current manuscript on leadership is published I will have sought and received critical comments from trusted friends and colleagues who will help make it better. The goal of a teachable spirit is to be better!

Humility produces tenderness in dealing with the failures or shortcomings of our peers and employees. Because we've received grace, we offer grace. For example, each time I'm tempted to become angry with an inept motorist who runs a red light or nearly hits me, I remember the times I have pulled in front of someone else. I have a mental picture of the day I changed my mind at the last minute and turned right instead of left out of my subdivision. I almost creamed an oncoming motorist. That flash and image is an abrupt reminder of my own frailty and fragility. Humbling, isn't it?

We need that grace because humility eludes a permanent grasp. We experience and find it operational in our lives, but all too quickly, we allow pride, arrogance, or independence to re-emerge and supersede it. The default mode of our human nature leans toward ego-centricity. Only after another episode that puts us in our place, do we return to an authentic perspective of humility.

Why is it that leaders who have an essential humility grow organizations that have lengthy positive trends? It's because *they build the organization to live beyond them and to exist without them*. They are more concerned about the best interest and health of the organization. Paul said it in Philippians: consider the interest of others as more important than your own. This kind of leader, who is under authority himself, is most capable to make the personal sacrifices to ensure the longer term viability of the organization. Unlike corporate raiders whose aggressive style cleans up the balance sheet at the expense of employees only to then sell the company for personal gain. The leader with humility thinks longer term.

In the first years of the founding of Calvary Baptist Church, I had a few people who occasionally asked me the question: what would happen to Calvary if I weren't here? To be sure, Calvary was closely identified with my leadership and many saw me as a significant driving force of our organization. Perhaps there were some tenuous times in those early days, and yet, there was no doubt in my mind that the structure we had put in place would provide for a continuing ministry beyond me. Our Leadership Team, by definition of our covenant, had all the authority (and the spiritual savvy) to competently guide Calvary. It was all there: the structure was clear, the roles were spelled out, the staff members were capable, and the vision had been cast. Calvary would have been fine. I look at our organization now, and after almost ten years of ministry, we still function under the same structure – long-term, forward looking, and adaptable – that will extend far beyond my tenure.

With humility, the leader assumes an approachable posture toward other employees and volunteers. Few things denote the health of an organization as much as the accessibility of the leadership. When there is the free flow of communication upstream and downstream, and when

> *Leaders with humility build the organization to live beyond them and to exist without them.*

employees feel validated by the consideration of managers and leaders, there's healthiness in the air. Little do we realize the incredible perception value of openness.

In an earlier pastorate, I didn't understand the perception that I communicated by my closed door (which didn't even have a window). Shockingly, I one day engaged in conversation with co-workers who began to joke about my "introversion," and how it appeared to them that I shut myself off behind my closed office door. I immediately had a window cut into the door and began to leave it open more often than not. That practice has continued. Today, I generally leave my office door open and I like nothing more than for one of my co-workers to stick their head in the door with a question. The perception has changed. A friend and co-worker told me he'd heard I was a good listener. That's what I'm looking for!

Humility helps one measure criticism and maintain sanity, especially when the darts fly and the venomous fangs are long and sharp. I've seen those cute signs like, "your best friend is your worst critic." And I don't agree at all. Most criticism is intended to do just what it sounds like - hurt! But if I start from the position of humility, I willingly acknowledge my weaknesses, oversights, and even failures. It's okay to wonder if there is there a shred of truth in the accusation that I can take away from it. Some leaders brag that they don't read anonymous letters. I, at least do that (just in case it's a bomb threat I need to know about) and then I evaluate if it's worth a second glance. I've found most have little to no merit, but occasionally I've gleaned something helpful.

The best criticism comes from those whom you know and trust. Though it may still hurt, you know the spirit of the person delivering the message. If you've developed the correct posture of humility then it can be a positive experience.

Humility is a powerful force in the life of a leader. Ironically, the person who evidences true humility has increased influence. Humility is not a manipulative ploy for power; it's an authentic means of relating to God and others. As you turn the page and digest the take away realities for this chapter, pause for a moment and reflect on this trait. Put yourself in the shoes of one of your co-workers or friends, and pretend that you are looking at yourself. What do you see?

Take Away Realities

- Humility is not a new leadership commodity, but is often overlooked as an essential for leaders.
- The nature of humility is: power under control, strength under submission, and pride subjected to restraint.
- Humility is an acceptance of the importance of others in our lives. In fact it's an acknowledgment that we need others. It's an admission that "I cannot do this alone."
- The person with humility is a receiver (allows others input) and has a teachable spirit, which are clearly strong indicators of humility.
- Humility produces tenderness in dealing with the failures or shortcomings of our peers or employees. Because we've received grace, we offer grace.
- Leaders with humility build the organization to live beyond them and to exist without them.
- With humility, the leader assumes an approachable posture toward other employees and volunteers.
- Humility helps us deal appropriately with criticism, whether it's constructive or destructive. The best criticism comes from those whom you know and trust.

Core Questions for Humility

1. Be honest, have you considered humility a critical component of leadership? Having now read this chapter, why should you include it?

2. Describe the negative connotations of humility (such as weakness) and based on your list, contrast the positive concepts that correspond to them. If necessary use the statement: Its very nature is power under control, strength under submission, and pride subjected to restraint. None of these phrases denote a weakly persona. They profoundly depict significant influence and authority that refuses to take advantage of others or to show arrogance.

3. The case is made in this chapter that "humility is an acceptance of the importance of others in our lives." Evaluate and reflect on your close relationships. To what degree do you allow those persons to have input into your life? How do you view them with regard to their investment and contribution to you? Do you see them as persons "to use" in pursuit of a goal?

4. How and why is it difficult for you to say: I need you, I cannot do this on my own?

5. If one mark of humility is a teachable spirit, gauge yourself on a scale of 1 - 10 with ten being the most teachable. If your teach-ability quotient is low, describe the steps you might take to improve.

6. Describe the connection between humility and a proper understanding of grace.

7. Consider your current organization: has your leadership prepared it to exist without you and

beyond you? If you were to cease leading right now, what would the organization do in the immediate future to stabilize its work flow and progress?

8. If you're in a management or leadership position, how would your employees describe your openness and approachability?

9. How does humility help you deal with criticism? Give an example of a recent critical comment and how it made you feel. How did you process it, and what did you learn from it?

A Core Case for Humility

A chief executive officer has a reputation for being aggressive, assertive, and insensitive to employees. Occasionally, a co-worker has stood up to her challenges and attempted to balance her "full speed ahead" charges. These confrontations have gone poorly and created more tension in the organization. However, the CEO has just attended a conference where the keynote speaker talked about humility as a core component of top tier leadership. His explanation and presentation was compelling and led to a few days of soul searching on the part of the CEO.

After returning to her organization, she called a meeting of her departmental leaders and apologized for her previous attitude and arrogance. She then asked for a frank assessment of how these managers viewed her leadership, and how she was respected by the employees in general. With this open invitation, the meeting evolved into a healthy discussion of the corporate culture, work environment, and a renewed vision for the organization.

    a. If you were the keynote speaker at the conference, what points would you include in a compelling presentation on humility?

    b. What's the level of risk this leader took in apologizing and initiating a frank discussion about her leadership? Do most organizations reward or penalize humility like this?

    c. How can this leader maintain a humble persona and not fall back into older habits of leadership? If you were this leader's mentor, how might you affirm the new direction?

d. Discuss the element and need for grace in a developing circumstance such as the attempted transition of leadership for this CEO.

CHAPTER 9

The Power of Intuition ...

Intuition is viewed with both suspicion and envy. Those who seem to have it are on the cutting edge of trends, and they somehow anticipate movements before others even catch a glimpse. We wish we could. It appears that something magical is in the air. How do they do it? What inside information might they have? Chalk it up to intuition, but not as a mystical or sixth sense kind of experience but rather the instinctual practice of pulling together disparate bits of information to discern a pattern or trend. We call it a "gut" feeling, but it's based more on barely perceptible clues that from experience we've been trained to see and compile. When structured into a portrait, we draw a conclusion.

It's very much like the three-dimensional posters that were popular some years ago. Upon first glance you could clearly see the top layer of the picture, but when you crossed your eyes or focused differently, a 3D image of a dinosaur, eagle, mountain range, or flag immediately popped into view. The images/clues are there, but it required learning how to see them. That's why intuition seems so mysterious to us. It's all there but some people "get it" and others don't, until they learn how to view the clues from a different perspective.

"Experience" is a major contributor to this ability. As a pastor for almost thirty years, I've come to recognize certain trends. I've seen the end results of certain shifts, movements, and even conflicts in the church. What might seem mysterious or baffling to a new pastor, I would recognize and understand since I've seen it a number of times. As a student of human nature, and having noted at times the worst of our behaviors, I can more easily pick up and discern when something is going right or wrong. I recognize the trends, I'm spiritually sensitized to these movements, and for me it's more about discerning the actions and end runs of people.

Since I have served Calvary for over a decade, I have gained insight into the seasonal fluctuations of attendance trends and typical responses of my congregation - some that are significantly unique to our church. A newcomer or outside observer may not detect these clues, but to me they are readily apparent. To develop this skill is a matter of watching and correlating cause and effect, or in my case observing and noting the particular characteristics of my fellowship. Intuitive people are persistent observers and learners.

A friend once described a situation to me whereby a church in another state manifested a particular dysfunction. The problem was specifically related to the leader of that congregation. As my friend gave me an overview of the situation and described the actions of the leader, I made the remark that it sounded as though the leader was attempting to hide something, maybe even a moral failure. The reactions of the leader to the threat of others in the church, and the attempts to manipulate meetings in the church led me to this conclusion. I had no direct knowledge of the individual's private life, but having seen similar behavior before, it seemed apparent that something was "not right." Guess what? Less than two years later the leader admitted to an affair and subsequently stepped out of his leadership role.

Intuition is the ability to read the signs and relationship between trends, circumstances and even people. Somewhere along the way, we diminish the capacity which we start with. As children, self-image comes from how others see us. It is the mirror in which we understand who we are, and it is conveyed by the facial expressions and verbal affirmations of those who care for and love us. So, appropriately, we learn to read those expressions and affirmations. Even as adults this can be true. The cues are there: the tone of voice, the crinkle of a smile, the slight moistness in the eyes, the tilted head. My wife and I can read each other's faces and verbal tones fairly accurately, and we can pick up on our sons' moods by the tenor of their voices. Long before we ask the question, "how are you doing" we've already made an assessment as to their emotional state of happiness or stressfulness.

In leadership, we do this all the time. We read a room, hear the intonation of a voice, and perceive how well our presentation is received from the feedback. We make minute adjustments in "what we say and how we say it" to better communicate our message. We gauge how far to go when confronting a difficult issue. We know when to stop short of hurting someone, or when to plow ahead because the door is open. We couch our arguments in terms that are best welcomed, and we soften our tones or conversely raise our voices when necessary. It's not a game, it's the process of reading the signs and cues and understanding the dynamics of that presentation or conversation. Yes, some of us are better at this than others due to any number of factors, but this is something we all do. And we can get better at it.

When assessing a situation, consider the issues inherent in the circumstance and think about the back-story that led to the crisis and the players who intersect that storyline. As an exercise visualize all the different pieces of the puzzle and reflect upon how they are related or how they influence one another. Ask someone to help you develop a different perspective or see the issue in a new light. Review the past history of your church or organization, and extrapolate that into a composite picture of a potential future based on current actions. Like the 3D picture that has multiple layers, when you look intentionally below the surface, you'll find the strands that tie it all together.

Thus, learn to evaluate and weigh the consequences of actions, attitudes, and decisions. A biblical model is the prophetic teachings of the Old Testament. A considerable amount of Israelite prophecy was predictive, based not only on future "foretelling" but on the consequential nature of prophecy. It forecasted that rebellion against the Lord would lead to dire ends; there were self-evident results of the people's failure to turn from their destructive ways. Simply explained, the consequence of destructive attitudes and actions were a destructive end. Duh! The principle applies to our consideration of intuition: when you acclimate yourself to the process of systemic cause and effect, the patterns will stick out more clearly.

For years in premarital counseling, I've taught about personality types and how best to understand the differences we have as individuals. The Myers-Briggs Type Indicator is one of the most widely known of these surveys or psychological tests. One of the eight preference polarities is known as "Intuitive." The person who is intuitive is not making speculative hunches or decisions by gut impressions, but has the ability to see connections and relationships that exist on a deeper level than the surface. The substrata meaning of those intertwined components inform the decision process. In practical terms, the leader makes decisions based on input from a variety of sources, compiles the data, and chooses a course – often doing so unconsciously. This is intuition.

Nowhere is this more necessary than when dealing with people, either in times of conflict or in the process of vision casting and inviting people to invest in that vision. Navigating through the land mines of people's personal biases and perspectives is challenging, and the ability of the leader to sidestep, adapt, reshape, recast, and then forge ahead is indispensable.

Regarding trends, intuition as a practicality can be based on understanding the cycle of growth and demise of an organization or a cultural fad. Sometimes, there are groundbreaking changes that occur and subsequently become the new norm. Seeing those changes as they are taking place in the category of people known as innovators, followed by early adopters, can provide some hints as to a future trend. Some decisions made by innovators and early adopters don't make it into the mainstream. But by watching what those persons are doing, you can sometimes catch a movement on the front end. Of course, not every trend is practical or profitable.

The book, The Blindside: Evolution of a Game, by Michael Lewis, presents the fascinating story of Michael Oher, who currently is a lineman for the Baltimore Ravens. Intriguing also, as the subtitle indicates, is the conceptual change made in professional football of the role and value (read money) of the left tackle's position. Long thought to be equal in importance, the left tackle among the linemen found new purchase power when professional football transitioned from primarily a running game to a passing game. The "blind side" of the quarterback was the left side, the off side of most right handed quarterbacks. The book further details the transmission downward of professional league trends through the collegiate to the high school level. For coaches and students of football technique, the changes in the NFL set the priorities for the lower levels.

The point is that trends usually begin somewhere, and those who appear to be intuitive are in large part just excellent students of cultural or organizational changes as they are taking place. They have the ability to implement appropriate changes in their own context. The intuitive person is one who has his eye on those who are further along than he is, and importantly, his finger on the pulse of his current environment. The intuitive person knows when and how to blend those two.

Take Away Realities

- Intuition is more likened to the instinctual practice of pulling together disparate bits of information to discern a pattern or trend.
- Experience is a major means of developing intuition, where we learn and are trained to see perceptible clues. We become skilled at correlating cause and effect.
- Intuition gleans the relationships between circumstances and trends.
- Asking and seeking others counsel and insight informs and extends your own intuitive capacity.
- Navigating through the land mines of people's personal biases and perspectives is challenging, and the ability of the leader to sidestep, adapt, reshape, recast, and then forge ahead is indispensable.
- The intuitive person is one who has his eye on those who are further along than he is, and importantly, his finger on the pulse of his current environment.
- The person who is intuitive is not making speculative hunches or decisions by gut impressions, but has the ability to see connections and relationships that exist on a deeper level than the surface.

Core Questions for Intuition

1. Does the concept of intuition seem magical to you? After reading this chapter, describe how you might see signs of your intuitive capabilities?
2. Identify a friend, mentor, or leader that you believe has significant intuitive insight. What leads you to that assessment, and how does that leader seemingly use his intuition?
3. Consider your vocational leadership position, what have you learned from experience and observation that an outsider might say are your intuitive observations?
4. What trends are currently developing in your organization? Project possible outcomes of those trends or circumstances?
5. If you are public speaker, describe an example of when you were able to read a room, and how that impacted your presentation. If you're not a speaker, reflect upon how closely attuned to a speaker you've noticed you were, and explain how the person tended to follow the lead of the audience.
6. Are there people in your life who can help you analyze a situation or trend, and coach you to increase your personal insight into that trend? Name a couple of these people and why they might be qualified to serve as a coach for you.

A Core Case for Intuition

After studying the ten year growth cycle of Central Church, the pastor has made some startling observations. Each Fall, there has been a general attendance trend upwards that continued through Christmas and peaked the following April, normally tipping downward right after Easter to the low point of mid-summer. However, this past year the Fall trend did not occur, and in actuality the numbers were flat until close to the next Easter, which showed a temporary spike, followed by the typical decline.

He compared the events calendar and noted several distinctions. In previous years, there had been a September Sunday School emphasis followed by an October Revival; both of which were not conducted in this year's cycle. The end result was that both Sunday School and worship numbers remained static, and the Wednesday evening programming showed a slight trend down. Further analysis showed that in eight of the last ten years, there had been new Sunday School units started each fall to anticipate the growth, and the Wednesday children's program had launched a musical production which was integrated into the Adult Christmas musical.

    a. Given that all other factors were similar, project and correlate the trends based on a comparative analysis.

    b. Apart from the obvious lack of the two main events, what other dynamics could have been in play? For example, reflect upon the spiritual impact of new Sunday School units and a Revival.

c. Based upon your understanding of the yearly cycle of your own church culture, what input would you give this pastor?

CHAPTER 10

The Power of Creativity ...

In discussing the intuitive process, there's a natural segue to the power of creativity. Intuitive people may be thought of as creative, but there's a wider berth to creativity than just being intuitive. For those who are like me and less spontaneously creative, this may be one of the most encouraging sections of this book – because yes, you too, can be creative!

For about sixteen years I've been involved in a group of pastors who meet monthly to share ministry concerns and pray together. Occasionally as one pastor leaves the group, we'll add a new person to the mix. Several years back, one of our long-term members was introducing us to the "new" guy by giving a one word description. When he described me, he attributed creativity as my identifying characteristic. Not normally thought of as a creative person, I was surprised and certainly appreciative of his comments. What I came to realize is that he saw in me certain abilities to think, envision, and work outside the normal boxes that we enclose ourselves in. He saw someone who prodigiously worked to create a new environment or culture in my organization, one who would challenge typical conventions. For me this is not spontaneous combustion, but is more about the process of thoughtful and artful calculations of current reality.

Creativity is not just about being "artsy" but can be found in many different venues. This statement didn't find fruition in my thought until several months ago when an outside reader of this project highlighted my creativity – in terms of organizational structure. Creativity is not restricted to paint on a canvas, water color on paper, decorating and design in a home, but it can be found in innovation and reinvigoration of an organization. To accomplish the creative goals of the leader, it usually takes much more methodical implementation than it does creative inspiration. As an author, I have often described the process of writing as 90% effort and 10% inspiration. Writing is a creative act and thus parallels this process well.

> As an author, I have often described the process of writing as 90% effort and 10% inspiration. Writing is a creative act and thus parallels this process well.

To be sure, there are those people who spring eternal with creative thoughts and energy. They seem to extemporaneously create *ex nihilo* (out of nothing). Though in reality, we understand that it is from the context of our experience and God-given hardwiring that creativity comes. Maybe our thoughts don't bounce off walls as the synapses rapidly fire or our quick wit stalls when our verbal acuity slows to a stutter, but that's okay because creativity doesn't have to be a hyped, A.D.D. experience. It can be the carefully thought through development of a concept – from inception to completion.

From my perspective, there are three legs on which creativity stands. The first is the Creator's stamp upon our DNA, whereby we become a reflection of Him in some unique way as individual people. In the Lord's economy of spiritual giftedness and creative dispersion, there are some who have unusual creative abilities, but everyone has some creativity. It can be expanded through disciplined effort and creating order for creativity. For instance, I'm able to accomplish much more when I put myself in the right environment and around the right people. Tremendous input can be obtained from listening to the ideas and thought process of others. Sometimes the energy spawned by a co-worker's or a friend's creativity will be the springboard for your own ideas.

Not long ago a conversation began as I asked about a friend's current projects. Listening to the overflow of his excitement, his unique perspective on the faith pilgrimage, and the God-sized projects he was working on, my thoughts flooded and ideas cascaded. His creativity fired my creativity and helped me raise my sights higher than my current expectations. Maybe there's a limit to how much ideation your mind will take before saturation, but regardless, hang around creative people, listen to the way they think, observe the process as it unfolds. It can be contagious.

Another component of the people dimension is to develop a group of people or find a trusted friend who can be a sounding board for you. Make it a safe place to bounce ideas around and to think way outside the box. Commit to the transparency and vulnerability this calls for, but in the longer view, the culling process of healthy feedback can save you much headache and the potential of a major train wreck. For some, the staff may serve as that repository of healthy discussion, while for others it may be people completely outside your realm of influence.

The second leg is temporal; creativity requires time. Some people work best when under pressure – good for them! I certainly get things done, but I flourish when I have time to process and reflect. For people like me who don't sprout an idea a minute, **time plus reflection increases creative potential**. I have to create space in my life in order to maintain a forward-looking thought process. Working from a "behind the curve" position cripples my capacity since I'm always catching up or putting out fires. These distractions serve to slow down my momentum and squelch my creative juices. Likewise for me, creating space is hard to do when the desk is covered with mail or stacked with folders: An ordered desk allows me to breathe mentally. If this can't be accomplished on a consistent basis, then a personal retreat is an excellent way to experience the "space" for creativity.

A third leg is the synthesizing of ideas - I'm a great synthesizer and refiner of concepts. Even if I don't have an inordinate amount of artsy creativity, I do have a significant ideation process. I can pull from many different fields of interest and areas of thought and fuse together

> *I read widely;, I observe broadly; I inquire steadily; I acquire comprehensively.*

a unique creative expression. I read widely; I observe broadly; I inquire steadily; I acquire comprehensively. From the varied fields of interest and endeavors I can see how certain components might fit together.

Calvary is an example of this assimilation process. When we founded Calvary Baptist Church, we took a fresh look at church structures and, in particular, synthesized ideas that I had been exposed to and set them into a new and fresh context. We asked the question: how can we accomplish the same functions or results but do so in a way that avoids some of the pitfalls of conventional church structures? The end result was an innovative structure that minimized the hierarchy, put more people closer to the ministries of the church with a comprehensive system of teams, and diminished the potential for disunity by dispensing with virtually all business meetings (among many other differences). These distinctions allowed the church to present itself as a creative and innovative organization, but more importantly provided the adaptability that was necessary for a young church. Interestingly, these same systems were designed from the outset to flex as the church grew. They are still fully in place now.

Each leader brings to the table a unique skill set, with traits weighted more in some areas than others. The wise leader is one who understands his own strengths and weaknesses and builds into his own system the stimulus for expansion in the ways needed. That development can come from personal growth or strategic building of a ministry team that complements the leader's repertoire.

Take Away Realities

- Creativity is not restricted to paint on a canvas, water color on paper, or decorating and design, it can also be found in systemic innovation and reinvigoration of an organization.
- Creativity stands on three legs:
  1. Your personal uniqueness and the input of others who surround you.
  2. Carving out time increases our capacity to create.
  3. Creativity includes the synthesizing of ideas. If you don't see yourself as an "originator" of ideas, then at least synthesize from others.
- Develop a group of people or find a trusted friend who can be a sounding board for you. Find a safe place to bounce ideas around and to think outside the box.
- Learn to recognize what environment fosters your personal creativity.
- Develop an ideation process that allows you to synthesize and pull from many different fields of interest. Read widely and fuse together a uniquely creative expression from the larger scope of things you're exposed to.

Core Questions for Creativity

1. List and describe the typical venues of creative expression. (for example: artist, sculptor.)
2. List areas that might fall into the category as artistic if you apply the broader definition as presented in this chapter. Detail why you've included them.
3. Consider the Creator's stamp upon your DNA, in what ways would you consider yourself to be creative?
4. Do you believe that creativity can be developed and expanded? Why or why not?
5. How does the right environment and people spawn creativity in you?
6. If it's true that creativity requires time, how well do you build time into your life and schedule to allow creativity to flourish? List a couple of strategies to change and increase your available time.
7. List other barriers or distractions to the development of your creativity.
8. Synthesizing ideas is a creative act. Are you reading widely, exploring new vistas, exposing yourself to new thought? List the books you've read recently. What could you do in the next few days that opens new ideas and thought for you? Think specifically about leadership in your vocation: who are the innovators, what are they doing, what are they writing?
9. What's your greatest creative limitation and how might you overcome it?

Mark W. Gregory

A Core Case for Creativity

Robert is a good leader: methodical, logical, and consistent in the decision making process. He's well respected among his peers and by his employees, but he's not generally thought of as a creative leader. It can't be denied that he's developed a solid organization that has been ahead of the game in a number of areas, and whose structure reflects an unusual approach for a not-for-profit group. Other community organizations have begun to notice the health and growth of his group, and several local leaders have asked him to conduct a seminar on successful non-profits. He's a little baffled by the invitation and why he should be the one leading this conference, but he acquiesced and agreed to do so. They have asked him to address two main lecture areas: creativity and organizational structure. He spent several weeks reviewing and developing his thoughts for the lecture, and in doing so he began to see a pattern that surprised him. He apparently was gifted at understanding organizational structures and how to build healthy systems. He also had to acknowledge that his curiosity drove him to explore and examine a number of national groups that were cutting-edge in their fields. He took the best of their ideas and implemented them in his group. Before the seminar, he asked a group of peers to give him a review of his lecture material. Their assessment was encouraging and revealing.

> a. On the basis of the chapter's presentation, what kinds of comments might his peer group make to him about the concept of creativity?

150

b. What limited his own understanding and perception of his creativity?

SECTION THREE

Organizational Nuances

"It always helps to start with a healthy organization;
one in which the vision is clear,
the involvement of the people is high,
the communication lines are open,
and goals are being met or surpassed."

CHAPTER 11

The Extreme Sport Of Change

Resistance to change is one of the chief sources of irritation that leads to organizational dysfunction. We should accept this as a reality and carefully work to shepherd the church through the strife that occurs. The wise leader starts with a basic assumption: change is inevitable! Even as hard as some might try to keep an organization static, that very act leads to the demise of the organization and introduces change. Can this change be avoided? My answer will surprise you: No, it cannot. Can it be managed: Yes!

Even in the healthiest of organizations, the very process of change introduces uncertainty, discomfort, and ultimately conflict. Yet, I do sense, as in a recent experience at my church, that change can have a lower level of discordant impact on an organization when certain elements are present or inserted.

It always helps to start with a healthy organization, one where *the vision is clear, the involvement of the people is high, the communication lines are open, and goals are being met or surpassed.* There's nothing like success to foster additional change. People are generally willing to concede to change when they feel it's

> People are generally willing to concede to change when they feel it's beneficial or successful.

beneficial or *successful*. Success is hard to argue with, and though certain markers of success may not always be authentic, success breeds success, and creates momentum.

From a non-spiritual point of view, momentum may be one of the strongest forces of a growth cycle in an organization. It's what turns the tide of the ballgame when one team makes a series of plays and everything is going their way. It's what attracts people, like bugs to light, when everyone hops on board and the organization burgeons with seemingly little effort. It stimulates interest and investment. Momentum is an intangible force that yields concrete results.

Conversely, the lack of it leads to a general malaise and in spite of the health of an organization, regaining forward traction for progress becomes painfully difficult. When an organization, like a cruise ship, slows and sits still in the water, the destination becomes a place that seems further away and delays the realization of the strategic plans. Furthermore, when a ship is still or drifting, it becomes more susceptible to the rocking of waves, eventually to be battered by the roiling of storm-level swells. When people perceive a ship is floundering, they abandon when the first raft hits the water. Actually, most abandon too quickly and become more a part of the problem, such as by attrition reducing needed resources, rather than assisting in a solution and reversing the trend.

The other side of the health spectrum is also true. Crisis regularly precipitates change and can make it more welcomed or sought after. When an organization descends to a level of significant pain or a terminal end, change is the only option. At this point, abrupt change is called for and accepted. There is an important role for incremental change, but at the point when the organization spikes low, change must be sudden like an intervention, signifying a reversal of trend. Often when you reinforce "crisis change" by validating the positive benefits and outcome, it becomes longer term or permanent.

The goal is to manage the change! Since change is inevitable, nudge it in the right direction through intentional and purposeful strategies. Use the necessity of change by casting vision for a different or better future. Involve people in the process, especially those who are leaders in your organization. Don't get so far ahead that they can't catch up. People don't normally like to be surprised, so lay it out appropriately.

Managing is not manipulating, which implies malevolent activity on the part of the leader, but rather it is putting in the right word at the right time, initiating a new policy at the correct moment, opening a door of opportunity that creates excitement, or making a personnel change that facilitates better results. This type of change management is more incremental, reflects continuous improvement, and results from outlining a healthy process and working through it with your fellow journeyers.

> *Communicate the "why" of change before you communicate the "how" of change.*

Communicate the Change! The first part of the process is to communicate the "why" of change before you communicate the "how." This extends your capacity for managing change if your members, participants, or

157

employees have an understanding of "why" their lives are impacted by your decisions. The "why" must *be reasonable, purposeful* and certainly *fit the organizational vision and goals*. If there's a perception that the reason for change has little bearing on the outcome or accomplishment of the goal, there's no incentive to be on board. To put this in perspective, I also realize and expect that people won't always agree or understand the *why* or *how!*

Here's an interesting twist on communication: *Process the change as a slow leak rather than a pressure break*. Work it through your leaders, then other selected individuals, then to the organization as a whole. At specific intervals, you can even give permission for the leaders and other informed persons to spread the word. I've found this to be healthy and effective. It accomplishes two things: first, you're not trying to hide the process. People don't generally like to have information hidden from them. Second, because news spreads quickly, when the process or procedures are announced it's more palatable since more people know about it and have been buzzing about it positively for some time. Use the process of a leak carefully, for truly, some things cannot be shared due to confidentiality.

Another part of managing and communicating the change is to help your employees or volunteers distinguish between message and method. In church life this is often stated: the message (the gospel) doesn't change, but the methods do. In many churches there have been fights over the type of music used in worship or in various ways of getting the gospel before a secular audience. Occasionally, though not always, I've had success by emphasizing our need to change the method to get the message into the vernacular of our day. In a secular organization, the end certainly doesn't always justify the means, but it can bring clarity to how to get there. Make it as painless as possible! Ask the question, "What's the impact on certain groups?" Then minimize the impact when you can. Find ways to maintain the normal experience of those who potentially could be inconvenienced the most.

The process and structure: When working through the process of change, it helps to identify the structure of the organization, consider which people need to be involved, and what process should be followed. Will it require a church or organizational vote, board approval, or does the leader have the authority to solely institute the change? Even if we believe we have the authority, it's not always advisable to start the process without significant people investing and approving of the changes. Having the right to do something is not the same as it being the right thing to do (it being a decision or action).

Identify the structure: If there is a structure in place, use it. In most churches there are traditional hierarchies such as deacons, elders, committees, and church councils. Most non-profits have some type of board, whether authoritative or advisory. Structures may be inherently neutral in their makeup, but there's no doubt that some tend to be more inefficient and cumbersome. The larger and more layered the structure, normally the longer it takes to work a decision through the system.

From the very beginning of Calvary Baptist, we decided to keep our structural system simple and the hierarchy very compressed. There are no committees, deacons or even a church council. We have invested authority in the teams that are closest to the ministry; with oversight from the Pastoral Team, the system has allowed us to adapt to the ministry needs as they arise. In addition, there is an appropriate check and balance with full oversight by our Leadership Team. The process allows us to make decisions quickly, change directions if needed, and consistently review the work of the church.

Whether complex or simple, the most important ingredient in the process is the level of trust and transparency that the leader has developed in relationship with the Church, Leadership Team, committees, or deacons. These two, trust and transparency, grease the wheels and precipitate decision making in a healthy manner. But the process is a two way street and competing agendas and power issues often derail the movement and the operating ability of the leader. In this case, there are really only three options: work the process through the current structure; change the current structure to better suit the ministry needs and vision of the church; or go around the structure – in essence play with the ones who want to play.

Since I've briefly addressed the first of the three, let me explain the second and third options. Changing the leadership structure of your organization or church may be a critical step if the decision making process has become so outdated or tedious that it's shutting down any forward movement. Assuming that the structure can be changed, the leader has to demonstrate why the old system is ineffective, why the new system is necessary, and what is the ultimate benefit of making the transition. Study other models of organizational structure. While considering your organizational heritage and tradition, look beyond the normal boundaries, denominational lines, and even into other fields of corporate culture.

A sequential plan for implementing the change, with target dates, intermediate steps, and a clear presentation may make the process more palatable. With the potential transformation of a structure, power and order is being shifted from one group to another. Be prepared, the ones who lose power are likely to protest and antagonize the transition. In the next chapter I'll deal more with conflict which you might encounter.

The third option is to go around the current structure, and play with the ones who want to play. This sounds more abrupt and adversarial than it has to be, and is not always a contrary defiance of the rule and order of the church. It can be as simple as getting permission to try something new and adding on to current ministries, while using people who want to participate. In this case it behooves you to minimize the adverse effect upon the organization.

For example, on one occasion years ago, I led a church to add on an extra worship service that was contemporary in nature. To best implement this, we worked hard to minimize the impact upon current members, hardly changing their existing schedule and ultimately streamlining their

> *Structure: work with it, change it, or go around it.*

Sunday morning time at church. To do this, however, I had to work around some of the structures and people who normally would have been responsible for certain experiences. So, I recruited people to lead and staff a second bible study hour and I personally led the worship team in planning and implementing the contemporary service. It added to my workload, but I placed no additional burden on the existing staff. Sometimes it's better to go around an existing structure than it is to create a doorway through it. I humorously refer to this principle frequently - play with the ones who want to play, and go around those who don't - to remind myself that occasionally you have to go a different route to achieve a goal. It also affirms that we should use those people in leadership who want to be a part of the future vision and direction of the church.

Understand the cost: Creating a new organizational culture or leading your group through a significant change may exact a toll upon you as leader. There's usually a price to pay, and you'll need to evaluate if you can survive changing the system and remain effective at the end of the transition.

There's no question that there are some hills worth dying on, but is the challenge confronting you worth the war? Keep in mind these two perspectives: First, at the end of the fight, will the church be in a better position and prepared for its future? Will its new culture truly reflect its mission and purpose and allow it to be effective? Or will the church be so wounded and weakened that it cannot move forward and perhaps even close its doors.

Second, if you don't survive the fight, are you prepared to make a personal transition into another position? You may have spent all of your reserves pushing something through, but subsequently have exhausted yourself emotionally and physically. Or you may have so alienated people that their resistance to the next step shuts down any further leadership potential you have. It's possible to lose the respect that is necessary to continue a beneficial role in the organization, and it's difficult to regain trust and respect again.

I know of many leaders who have gone through extreme battles and though they, themselves, did not survive the war, the church was better prepared for its future. Sometimes, the leader who expends himself doesn't see the results, and it's the next pastor that reaps the harvest. In essence, the first guy paid the price, and the second guy gets the reward – seems unfair but it happens. But, there are others who carefully evaluate the process, envision an end point, survive the transition, and subsequently they lead the church beyond the crisis point and into a wonderful future. Just know what you're getting into!

Timing and pacing the change: Be sensitive to how much change the church or organization can take and how quickly it can take it. It's a little like reading between the lines, but you can discern and gauge how fast to go. It's a matter of pressure. When you shake someone's hand, you know how hard to squeeze without hurting the person. In our martial arts ministry, when we teach self-defense moves to our karate students, they learn how much pressure is needed to subdue someone without hyper-extending an elbow or wrist. A leader can only push so far and so hard before the pain becomes intolerable and people start pushing back. When a leader knows and cares about the members of his organization, a relationship develops that informs the push and pull of change.

There's usually an ebb and flow to the pace that a leader can exert. Sometimes it's a seasonal phase and a strategic step that requires you make a major transition at a particular time in the year. In our church, there are two distinct times in the yearly cycle when it's best to implement a transition: At the beginning of the year and in the late summer/early fall, about the time summer vacations wind down and the school year starts. We usually see a significant trend upwards at both of those times. For us, there has normally been a discernable decline that starts in mid to late April, and hits the low point around the second week in July. Why? Spring baseball, school ending, and summer vacations. Yet, with school restarting in late July and August, the family schedule stabilizes and the trend-up maintains a fairly consistent growth pattern. January is almost always strong for us, and we expect to get a bump in attendance at that time.

Logistically, if we are to make changes and transitions, we need to time it to correlate with these cycles. This requires us to back up the time line for weeks or even months of preparation and communication of the "why" and "how" of the change. By that time, we trust people are ready and hopefully willing to go along. Seasonal cycles may be different for various organizations, but each has a particular time-stamp of trends. Watching, knowing, and utilizing these can help turn a strategy into a positive trend.

Also, sensitive leaders can detect when there is a general movement for change that is developing among the people. There are times when your congregation or members are ahead of you in seeing or expressing a need for "something" to happen. This is good, and a smart leader listens, factors in the overall strategy, and synthesizes a plan that incorporates the goals of the organization and the interests of the people.

Another principle of pace is after every hard push, take a breather. Give people a chance to recover, regain their equilibrium and stop wobbling from the trauma of the recent changes. As a runner I often do interval sprints to increase my level of conditioning. After each interval, a slow down period allows me to recover so that I can push again, and ultimately raise my physical capacity. Add to that, there is a need for your body to recover after a long run such as a marathon or half-marathon. Organizations are just like our bodies, they are organisms that must have stages of rest and recovery. Creating temporal space and breathing room helps prepare people for another phase. I've observed after a hard push that a period of unwinding stabilizes the organization, releases some pressure, and sets you up for another season of growth.

At some point, the process of change will either slow down and fizzle out, or it will build momentum and roll through barriers and obstacles. In writing my first fiction novel, I had always said that if I reached a certain point (around eight chapters), I knew I could finish it. It was the tipping point of "I can do this" and where I could more clearly see the end of the book. Once I had that in sight, I just had to fill in the blanks. Occasionally in working through the organizational hoops of change, you may reach a place of stasis. It's a tough spot and is emotionally and physically draining. Keep in view the greater picture, and persist in a manner that is appropriate for your people. Be sensitive to the culture of the group, but nonetheless hang on to the vision and push through the tipping point.

Once you've carried an organization through the process of change, don't look back or vacillate toward a reverse course. To do so carries the organization through pain once again. Stay the course until the process of change is complete, or at least until you reach a place of such great discomfort that you have to scale it back a little. There are those rare times when a side step or a temporary reprieve might be necessary if your church is confronted with an extreme crisis. The difference is similar to a balloon; when grasped and squeezed it will compress and respond to the pressure, but it will burst when a pin is pressed against it. Learn the difference between healthy pressure and the crucible of an abrupt break. It might save you from pushing too far.

To bring together the many parts of this chapter, consider how inevitable change is for all of us. We grow from infancy and mature to adulthood, and then we begin to detect the encroaching effects of aging. Change happens, but the crucial element is how we manage that change. I just completed an annual medical physical and got a great report, but nestled in the exam and lab work are the middle age realities of my need to manage my future health. Attention to my personal change process will enable me to have great expectations for the future years of my life.

Our organizations will invariably morph with the march of time, and a part of a wonderful future for our churches will be determined by our successful leadership as we carry them through a healthy change!

Take Away Realities

- Change is inevitable, so manage it.
- Crisis can be a precursor to significant change.
- Communicate the "why" of change before you communicate the "how."
- One strategy is to communicate the change as a slow leak rather than a pressure break.
- Identify the organizational structure: work with it, change it, or go around it.
- Time the changes that are necessary based on the normal yearly cycles of your organization.
- Pace those changes with sensitivity to your people, but with appropriate pressure to move the organization forward.
- Consider the cost to your group and to yourself as you evaluate and implement needed changes.
- Once you've worked through the process of change, don't vacillate or reverse the change, unless you hit a major crisis or break point.

Core Questions for Managing Change

1. Consider the organization you lead or in which you participate: is it already in transition or in a place of stasis?

2. Identify the most immediate issues and needs that might precipitate and provide incentive for change.

3. What means and media does your organization use to communicate change? How well are you communicating the "why" of change as compared to the "what" of change?

4. If you were to communicate change as a slow leak, discuss the concentric spheres of people you would involve in the process.

5. What type of structure does your organization have: traditional, innovative, complex hierarchy, compressed hierarchy? Then discuss whether the structure is conducive to the change process or restrictive of it.

6. Reflect on the three-part structural process: work with it, change it, or go around it. Which of these would be the most viable for your leadership and the current structure of your organization. List the advantages and pitfalls of each.

7. Gauge the level of trust that you have as a leader in relationship to the larger structure of the organization as well as with the general members. If the trust level is low, how might you improve it?

8. Based on the current change needs of your organization and a clear understanding of what the

future should bring, could you survive the process? Why or why not?

9. Identify and list the normal yearly cycles of your group. How do needed changes coincide with those cycles? How much pressure can you put on your people?

10. If you've pushed through a critical time of change, describe how you've allowed the people to have some breathing room and recover. If you've not done this, reflect on the potential benefits for your organization to pace the changes.

11. If you've gone through significant change, how have you been tempted to look back or go back? Would it further disrupt the organizational culture? How might you lead the people to look forward rather than back?

Core Cases for Considering Change

Case Study 1: A church that once had run close to two thousand in worship attendance has diminished to an average of four hundred each Sunday. The facility is large and there is a significant amount of debt. The city, however, continues to flourish and the potential for outreach and growth is good. A new pastor has been on the scene for ten months and is now acclimated to the community and church cultures. His first goal has been to get to know the people and build rapport with the current leadership structure, and his assessment is that progress is being made. The pastor and leadership are now introducing sweeping changes to salvage the finances and reverse the growth trend, including the following: cutting ministry budgets, reducing personnel by utilizing more part time employees, and launching an aggressive advertising program through newspaper, television ads, and web presence.

> a. How might the leaders best communicate the needed changes? What process would you suggest to demonstrate to members the necessity of these changes?
>
> b. What other steps might be necessary to reinvigorate the church's ministry?

Case Study 2: A medium-sized church in a town of 40,000 people has not grown in at least ten years. It's stuck on a plateau, fluctuating between 250 - 300 in attendance. The pastor has been there five years and is well educated, reads widely on the subject of leadership, regularly attends church growth conferences. Yet, most of his ideas for outreach and innovation are not adopted by the church. In fact, it hardly gets past the leadership structure which fire-hoses his initiatives and limits his authority. He finds there is some support in the church for his vision, but most of these persons are not in leadership positions in the church.

      a. Using the concepts of organizational structure as outlined in this chapter, develop possible scenarios based on: 1. work with it, 2. change it, or 3. go around it.

      b. Consider how much church and personal cost is involved in each of those three.

CHAPTER 12

———

Full Contact – Conflict Management

Conflict really does feel like a contact sport! The blows are hard even if they are verbal. The schisms run deep and the wounds refuse to heal. Conflict often burns hot, then subsides temporarily until new fuel is added to the flame. At times it scalps the landscape and leaves catastrophe and rubble, signaling the end of an organization. Often, though, conflict is a precursor to new development and change; it cleans away the old weeds and underbrush that stunts growth and allows fresh foliage to emerge.

It's a given that every group will have some level of conflict. The healthiest ones deal with it appropriately and move beyond it quickly. Others persist and languish in it until they become labeled as difficult organizations. I've known of some churches that have developed the reputation of a "troubled church," and their cyclical pattern of hiring and firing pastors, having bad business meetings, and making a public show of their private business is disgraceful to the kingdom. Yes, there is a better way! And it begins with a careful analysis of the conflict as it comes to your attention.

The first level of attack is to gauge the severity of the conflict. Initial questions I normally want to answer are: what's the nature of the conflict and who's involved in it? Is it about the leader: a decision that he has made or some personality quirk that caused friction. If the leader is not directly involved then the process will probably unfold differently.

Some issues demand an immediate response due to their volatile, accusatory, or even legal nature. You may find that some reported conflicts are nothing more than misunderstandings and can be reconciled by a phone call or a "sit down" meeting. I've learned it's best to gather information about a conflict from more than one person or angle, though this is not always possible. Multiple confirmations can provide insight and keep you from bulldozing through a situation when all that was needed was clarification. Conflicts take on a life of their own and will escalate proportionately to the attention given them. Let's make sure it's really a battle worth fighting or a fire worth fueling.

Who is involved? Does the conflict involve core people, or those who are on the periphery of the organization? Are the people habitual "pot stirrers" or "rabble rousers"? Core influencers have more leverage and consequently can do more damage. This raises the stakes for the leader and inherently causes more pain. People who are more peripheral can still cause stress and grief, but their impact doesn't have the same mass to produce force and movement. There are some people who really love a fight; for them it's an adrenaline rush and a way to flex their muscles. It gives them a feeling of control and importance. Ironically, these same people may be powerless in their vocation or home, but somehow the church is the one place where they can have their say. The church, in its innocence and desire for equality, often gives a platform to people who would not normally have such a means of voicing complaints.

A third level, then, is to ascertain how widespread the conflict may be. If the conflict is confined to a subset of the organization, contain and quarantine it there. Deal with the issue and the people on the level that is most appropriate (preferably the lowest possible level). Realize that the higher the level you deal with the conflict, the greater the potential for negative impact on your organization. The ability to catch it quick and "nip it in the bud" is a great strategy, provided that your action doesn't create a greater problem.

Before there is a huge public showdown, there is merit in working behind the scenes. When there is misunderstanding, a few well placed conversations to promote clarity have often saved the day in a crisis. It's something I refer to as "running interference," and it sometimes allows you to serve in a facilitating and reconciling role. The danger is that you potentially become a participant in the conflict rather than a more neutral observer. You may also be perceived as forming a judgment before all the details are known.

> *Realize that the higher the level you deal with the conflict, the greater the potential for negative impact on your organization.*

Very few people really win if the conflict occurs in the public arena. Factions develop; sides are chosen; undercurrents rip people apart; old issues re-emerge. All bets are off by the time an issue gets to a public and messy business meeting, or an interoffice drama. Knowing on what level and how quickly to deal with an issue is admittedly an art form honed and sharpened by previous trial and error. One way to approach a conflict is to consider, "if left alone, will it get better or worse?" We often add fuel to the fire when we barge in and attempt to fix something that really has few consequences and is a minor issue. We may accelerate the problem when we don't have all the information and jump too quickly to conclusions.

A conflict is like an iceberg, the tip is showing but with most of the mass underneath the surface. I have learned the hard way that there are a lot of details left out when people explain their perspective and participation in a conflict. It is human nature to paint ourselves in the best light. In conflict, it's often a perception war, based on the facts that are known, rather than what's not known. In reviewing and reflecting on conflict issues, I repeatedly affirm to myself and others that "there's a lot more going on here than we can see at this point," or "there's more to this story than we know." Sometimes, only years later, have I discovered (or someone revealed) a critical piece of information that shed light on what was really happening in the conflict.

Confidentiality is critical when addressing conflict. It helps to contain the conflict and protects employee's reputations. There are few things more debilitating to an individual than to have an unfair or undeserved accusation hanging over them in the work environment. The perceptions of other employees are important in creating equity and positive interactions.

> *The reality is that many conflict decisions are made on the basis of "inside" or "confidential" information ...*

Dealing with conflict is not an individual or isolated process but involves many people, including other leaders who are integral to the organization. In my case, I have a Leadership Team that I'm accountable to, as well as from whom I receive beneficial counsel. For many of the conflicts that I've dealt with, this team has been an insightful peer council that collectively processes the issues and makes decisions about actions or reactions. If we, or I, make a decision that is not easily understood and misinterpreted, it's important and helpful to have the strength of others to stand with me. The reality is that many conflict decisions are made on the basis of "inside" or "confidential" information that cannot be shared with the organization (church) as a whole. But with the broad respect and integrity of my Leadership Team, the church gives credibility to our decision, and trusts that we have dealt fairly and appropriately.

There will be casualties with any conflict. Even when you successfully deal with an issue and have been sensitive to the participants, there will almost always be a winner and a loser. While some resolutions are win-win, a great deal of conflict resolution still leaves someone with an advantage and the other party with a concession. Hurt feelings and perceived injuries often lead people to forsake your organization. It's a part of life. Attempts to relieve the hurt and pain are appropriate but not always successful. Be aware going into the conflict that this will happen, and be determined to maintain your integrity, but also expect that you will lose some people along the way. It's painful but true, sometimes losing people actually opens the door to the next level of growth and healing for your organization. Be at peace and let them go in peace.

Truly, though, most of us want to minimize the exodus that results from a conflict. The manner in which you conduct your leadership will alleviate some of the blood loss. If people know your integrity and clearly see your heart motives, they may be more inclined to stay. Presetting ground rules for potential conflict may minimize the tension as you deal with issues. For years, I have conducted premarital classes where I teach young couples these principles and how to deal with conflict. First, know that conflict will happen. Second, build the healthiest of relationships, which are better equipped to deal with the blips that hit the screen. Third, determine in advance how you'll fight. Here's a few from a sample list:

1. Don't involve in-laws in your battle
2. Take a break if the emotional level escalates toward physical confrontation
3. Use words that describe your feelings, not accusations of the other's fault
4. Ask the question, "What's really going on here?"

I usually assign them homework to write out their own rules. Transferring this to an organizational level, we can prescribe some elements that help diffuse the emotion of a business meeting or confrontation. One example: rather than a structured business meeting, plan smaller informal group meetings that can be led by a respected leader; establish how questions will be fielded and what's off-limits or of such a confidential nature that it can't be discussed; and carefully monitor and deflect personal attacks. Keep things on the level of principles. While this is just one example, it's clear that there are ways to keep the pressure low. Sometimes, changing the venue of the meeting can be a huge deterrent.

As a result of the casualties of a conflict, on a number of occasions I have conducted "exit interviews," from which I usually glean helpful feedback. Sometimes the critiques are hard to hear and are personally directed to me as a leader. Often they are biased if the person left because of unmet expectations (whether realistic expectations or not) or from some disrupted relationship in the church. Use appropriate filters and discernment when necessary, but always ask: "Lord, what would you desire to teach me from this conflict or this personal conversation?" You'll find every conflict to be a learning and humbling experience.

The way in which we as leaders manage conflict says a lot about our integrity, character, and ultimately how successful we may be within that environment. If we keep the spiritual nature of our work at the forefront of our actions, and have sensitivity to the people who are involved in the conflict, we are more likely to sustain our leadership in that organization.

Mark W. Gregory

Take Away Realities

- It's a given that every organization will have some level of conflict. The healthiest organizations deal with it appropriately and move beyond it quickly.
- Consider the following: Gauge the severity of the conflict. Who is involved? How widespread is it? Are there confidentiality issues in dealing with the people in the conflict?
- Deal with the conflict on the level that is most appropriate, preferably the lowest possible level.
- There will be casualties in almost every conflict.
- You can survive conflict!

Core Questions for Conflict Management

1. Do you agree that conflict is inevitable in an organization? Defend your answer.
2. Have you been in a major conflict, in one right now, or know someone who is? If so, write out a summary of the primary issues and how long you (or they) have been dealing with them. Answer the following questions:
   - What's the nature of the conflict?
   - Who are the primary players?
   - How widespread is the conflict?
   - Must it be addressed now?
   - At what level does it need to be tackled?
   - How public is it?
   - What are the consequences of dealing with it, or leaving it alone?
3. In your organization is there a process and mechanism already in place for dealing with conflict? Describe how it works.

Mark W. Gregory

A Core Case for Conflict Management

It's a mess. The pastor had not paid close enough attention to the storm that was brewing. As the breeze whipped into hurricane force winds, he realized that the surge was now licking at neck level. It started as a minor complaint in a small side ministry of the church. Unfortunately, it was the pet ministry of the unofficial power broker in the church.

The pastor got wind of it first in a committee meeting when a member pulled him aside to tell him that feelings were hurt and people were saying, "The pastor didn't care about that ministry." A quick phone call to the people involved added fuel to the fire when he refused to stand up for the broker who wanted to allocate budget money to the project. The quarterly business meeting was scheduled for one week from today, and he knew that the ministry issue would come up and assume center stage. "How did it get to this?" he asked himself. "It's such a petty matter!"

a. In what ways did the pastor miss the signs of the significance of the crisis? To your best understanding of the case scenarios, answer the questions listed above, such as, what's the nature of the conflict? Who are the primary players?

b. What steps could he take now to circumvent a bad business meeting, or to diffuse the anger of the power broker?

c. Analyze how petty issues become major crises.

CHAPTER 13

Muster The Troops
Personnel Management

There are few things more rewarding or more frustrating than the personnel side of leadership. Seminary couldn't have begun to prepare me for the reality of being a human resources officer, organizational administrator, and pastor, all in one. It's the side of leadership that requires consistent nurturing, and demands more time and energy than I feel I have to give. On occasions, I have functioned more like a moderator or arbiter of interoffice conflicts than a leader of a cohesive unit. As a friend of mine often says, it's like "herding cats." And yet, somehow, the group keeps moving together in the same direction.

It's critical that everyone is working together and pulling in the same direction. There are many benefits to this, one of which is less dissention and griping. Another friend frequently said, "pulling mules don't kick." To expound on his humorous statement, it's my assessment that those who are a part of the process, who are committed to the health of the organization, and who are working to achieve the goals of the group, are less likely to kick against the *goad*. How great it is when everyone on board shows up and fulfills their responsibility with passion and a positive attitude.

One summer, my family had the opportunity to go on a cruise. We were far back in the credentials line and subsequently late in boarding the ship. As we pulled our luggage onto the elevator to go up to our room, the muster call sounded. For those who haven't yet been aboard a ship, the muster call is the emergency drill where the passengers proceed to an established lifeboat post with their flotation jackets and rehearse the safety procedures. I cordially remarked to a person getting off the elevator, "I guess we'll miss the drill." His quick response set me straight, "No, everyone does the drill." He was correct. We dropped our gear in our cabins as the attendants were clearing rooms, making sure everyone responded. When we arrived at the lifeboat on deck seven, people were lining up and being checked by the mates. They were serious. It wasn't over until every single person had shown up at their posts, every name crossed off the list, everyone had a life jacket, and everyone ran through the emergency procedures. What a lesson about everyone being on board and at their stations with the purpose and goals of the organization! It's a basic expectation of those who are called together to achieve something great, by everyone doing their part and everyone moving the same direction.

It begins with the assembling of a team – more often called the hiring process – and the crucial need is to put the right people in the right places. It begins with the "who" factor. Many of us have looked over the resumes and evaluated the credentials of the applicants. Really, what do we expect from that? Resumes are geared at putting the best foot forward. At best it's an initial culling method, but it only gets us and the candidates onto the playing field. Skill sets and educational experience are important, but that's only the first base of hiring. The current trend among many larger churches is to hire from within, wherein they know the person, they've seen the individual function in the corresponding ministry environment, and they have had the chance to observe the character of the individual. This certainly gives you a heads up. But most of us don't have that luxury and have to start with a piece of paper, followed by referrals and recommendations. Yet, we can still value the same components. We can discern the character of the person from lengthy conversations with references and by initial interactions with the prospective candidate.

I've more recently turned my attention to the following thoughts: Are these persons teachable and does their persona reflect humility? Do they have a quality of character that reflects the organization? What relational skills and strengths do they bring to the table? How about creativity – is that a desirable need for the particular job? Do they seem compatible with the current staff? Conversely, are they abrupt and demanding? Do they have a reputation of being a loose cannon, or of disregarding the authority of their boss? Unfortunately, these statements tend to be more subjective than objective, but you can still learn a lot from interviews with the references and subsequently the formal interview process within your organization. The point is that you're looking at broader criteria than the basic credential screenings.

I also attempt to get a wide base of involvement from people who are serving in the respective areas of ministry. By exposing the candidate to more people and getting feedback from them, you're better able to gauge basic compatibility and sometimes discover a red flag along the way. This fulfills an ancillary function as it gives people in your organization an opportunity to be a part of the process, and thus invested in the welfare of your workplace.

In a volunteer situation, where you have people offering to serve on teams, you have to consider two components: the strength and ability of the team leader, and the compatibility of team members. There needs to be a clear delineation of who is leading. Often in volunteer positions, there can be jockeying for position that's unhealthy and detrimental to the effectiveness of the team. In our situation, because of an open team structure, we appoint the team leaders and we rely upon each person as our "go to" man or woman.

Once your team is assembled, then begins the process of "herding those cats," beginning with expectations, motivation, and reinforcement. Like flour in the cake, expectations are the basic component in the recipe for a healthy team. Expectations are on two levels: First, the larger corporate level where we define vision, goals, and benchmarks (in that descending order). If the team member has bought into the vision and goals, then by spelling out the intermediate benchmarks, it gives an indication of "what's my part in this plan?" which is the second level. Employees and team members work better when they know what's expected of them. There's nothing more frustrating than fulfilling a task, and later finding out it didn't matter or wasn't what you were supposed to do. The role of leader is to help guide an employee or team member by providing those expectations. (I'm not referring to a job description, which, if not done properly, can limit the scope and work of members.) More specifically, expectations are based on "what role" this person plays in moving the organization toward the benchmarks. That role may have very specific requirements, as referenced in a job description, but roles are larger than a list of "to do's."   So, there is a direct correlation between roles and expectations. Expectations must be frequently revisited and occasionally redefined. That's normal, for as an organization reaches certain benchmarks, it adapts and changes to push upward to the next level.

Where does motivation come from? We might assume that motivation is primarily an external stimulus, such as financial incentive or fear of losing a job. Motivation is probably based more on personal values or in a belief in the organizational

> *Motivation occurs when "it matters to them."*

future. I'm often asked, "How do you motivate volunteers?" My initial thought is that a stirring and rousing speech is what really gets people going. But I'd have to acknowledge that's only partially true. Motivation occurs when "it matters to them;" and for some, the money, job security, or desire to please, does matter. For others, such as volunteers, that's not enough. Motivation can be created and enhanced by the speech and actions of a leader, but it has to touch the core of what that person believes or wants for the organization. So, the first point of motivation is to sell and highlight what the organization is all about and make a personal connection between the person and the organization.

Motivation comes by observation of added value to an organization or when members see results of their efforts. In spiritual terms, there's great motivation in seeing lives transformed through your work and ministry.

Financial incentive can't be overlooked as a motivating factor. For the person who is just doing a job, punching a clock, then financial leverage is strong. The old adage is appropriate: some people work to live and others live to work. And for those who work to live, finances are a huge motivator.

Performance reviews are of some benefit, especially in a corporate environment where financial incentive and job retention is a key component. Likewise, if you have a truly healthy work environment and you're respected as a leader, then a periodic performance review can be affirming and can provide a constructive critique that really benefits the employee. If a person understands that their job is not on the line, they're more open to hearing constructive comments.

Peer reviews can work if the environment is healthy, but I've seen some office cultures where peer reviews would have been very counter-productive. Here, the determinate factor is the level of healthiness or dysfunction that is currently operational in your environment. To put a finer point on it: do you have an individual that causes dysfunction and would sabotage or skew the healthy process of a peer review? If so, this type of evaluation could cause great distress and disharmony. Avoid it until the environment can handle appropriate interactions.

Guess what doesn't work for volunteers – leverage through financial incentive.   Ah ha! So then what does? Expectations are still important. If an individual has "bought in," and has a connection in their personal values to the organization, then creating, communicating, and even raising expectations will often bring positive results. The opportunity to move into greater responsibility can be a point of leverage for some. For others, consistent encouragement is all that's needed. Motivation can be reinforced by reward, which can come in many ways, though there should always be positive verbal reinforcement of a job well done. In the end, however, you must be prepared to talk straight with the volunteer, just like the paid employee, with the hopes of obtaining greater performance.

A "dialogic follow up" is the method I've developed for follow up and reinforcement. Admittedly it's based on my relational strengths and the positive conversations I have ongoing with my staff, but it's a good model. It means that you maintain running conversations with your key employees or team members about the direction and effectiveness of their work.

In my office, we've developed a strong rapport and it allows us to stay in frequent and consistent communication about what's happening. The initial portion of our weekly staff meeting is spent with all the office employees, followed by concentrated time with the ministerial staff. In the smaller meeting we discuss pending issues, progress, new concepts, and generally stay on top of the overall ministry. Beyond that, I do a "hit and run" with them, whereby I catch them in their office or they drop by mine, and we more fully discuss trends and goals.

I recently learned when we reviewed this book in staff meetings, that at first they were unsure of my "drop in" questions, such as "How do you feel your ministry is going?" or "In what areas would you like to see personal improvement?" From previous experiences they had determined those kinds of questions were threatening or a prelude to a critical critique of performance. As they learned to trust me and to recognize this was my way of helping them think through the processes of their ministry, the questions took on a different perspective. No longer intimidating, the "starter questions" are a means of dialoguing about the realities of our ministries and how to move through points of stasis, personally and professionally.

Because I tend to be more "hands on", my staff consistently runs ideas by me before launching into a new area of ministry. The ongoing dialogue is the means by which I give direction and feedback. Ultimately this frees them to make minor course corrections or to experiment with a new idea without the fear that the repercussions are grave. We are able to keep pressing and moving forward incrementally and sometimes exponentially.

> In encouraging, affirming, or even correcting those we work with, it's a good idea to make many smaller steps along the way rather than big jumps all at once.

The Japanese car industry has a term, *kaizen*, which means *continuous improvement*, the process of making many smaller adjustments and corrections until a product has reached the standard of excellence. In encouraging, affirming, or even correcting those we work with, it's a good idea to make many smaller steps along the way than big jumps all at once.

A last note regarding personnel: Yes, there is a time for termination or bringing a less abrupt, but healthy close, to an employee's or a volunteer's tenure. In the leadership classes I teach, I'm frequently asked about my mistakes as a leader. I'm willing to concede there are many. Among the more remarkable occurrences, one that I often refer to is summarized like this: *Hiring poorly and firing too late.* I've made some great decisions about staff, but I also allowed myself, against better judgment, to hire persons about whom I felt uncertain. Invariably, the decision ended in a difficult situation and presented a learning opportunity for me.

I've seen the "lines drawn in the sand" when an employer reaches the point of termination, and I've heard and rehearsed the best ways to speak to an employee about difficult situations. After many years of listening to mentors and friends, experiencing the process, or seeing other leaders make difficult decisions, I've reduced the paradigm to the following three statements.

So, how do you know when to terminate?*

- When it's best for the employee: The employer is the one who makes the determination, and unfortunately, there is seldom agreement

---

* Review and adhere to applicable state and federal regulations regarding employment practices and guidelines. Some states have employment-at-will laws, others do not. Use caution to comply with your church, corporate, educational, or business policies. Consult an attorney concerning an appropriate process of termination.

between the employee and employer. The different perceptions about the person in a particular capacity and their job performance can fall into a debate over opinions. Avoid this by keeping a record of conversations, documenting performance reviews, and maintaining other personnel file information. From the employer's perspective as an objective observer, there are times when it's apparent that the employee isn't satisfied, fulfilled, or matched well with their work. This disparity creates resentment in the employee or at best a begrudging attitude toward their work and business environment.

- When it's best for the organization: Since effective personnel are critical to achieving goals, even an average employee can cause delays or gaps in the time line of reaching a benchmark. Unproductive employees sap resources that could be used or reallocated in other ways. There may be longer term strategies that require certain skill sets or an increased leadership capacity, and it's clear the current employee is not capable of making the journey. It may be possible to structurally reorganize and allow the employee to fulfill a different function in the organization. The end point is to evaluate and balance the question of what's best for the employee and employer.

- When an employee becomes a detriment to the health of the work environment: The toll is not just on the effectiveness of their personal work, but also on the ability of others to do their jobs well. When left unattended, it often creates a dysfunctional environment that spreads systemically throughout your organization. A poisoned or negative worker clouds the interactions of the team as a whole, and can lead to clusters of employees with subterfuge and maneuvering. It's clearly a detriment to the organization when poor work performance cannot be corrected, especially if there's been a constructive attempt to up the expectations and help the employee develop better habits and attitudes.

If you're in a volunteer organization or you're leading a team, you can plug in some of the above dynamics for your group. Evaluate whether a member is helping or hurting the process of attaining the goals. The same principles apply, though the exit strategy for the volunteer may be significantly different.

It's hard to terminate an employee, and in church life it's even tougher since we intentionally cultivate an atmosphere of grace. Occasionally employees take advantage of it. If possible, ease the employee out, by helping them find the right job, or by giving them ample time to find a new employer. There are those times where you may have to draw a line and release the employee abruptly. The validity of making these hard decisions can be evidenced by the refilling of a position with the right person who moves the organization to the next stage.

It's important to distinguish between performance and personhood. If we take corrective action with an employee, it helps if we present our case from the perspective of tangible behaviors or tasks that are not tied to personality. We can address skills by providing more training. We can re-define a role by expanding the expectations, or we might be able move the person to a different spot in the organization that better suits their abilities. In all of these attempts, we should refrain from making accusations against personalities.

But what do you do if you have hired someone who has a difficult personality? It happens. You may not spot it immediately, but after a while, you begin to observe characteristics that concern you, such as: manipulation, passive aggressive behavior, criticism, or laziness. First, evaluate how much havoc the person is creating and gauge your level of tolerance. I sometimes refer to this as the "dance", where you have to work around someone, or even consider how best to phrase a task request, because you expect resistance. Do other team members prefer to do something themselves rather than asking the person to do it, even though it might be their job? The dance occurs when people keep their distance from the individual, and they feel as though they're walking on egg shells when interacting with this person. It happens when you're worried about what might set them off. It's awkward. Uncomfortable. And unproductive.

Second, address the situation, but not in a public setting that creates a spectacle or escalates the tension. I do think it's a good idea to have someone join you in that conversation so that it doesn't become a "matter of opinion"; you have a secondary verification of the behavior that's causing the problem. If you have a difficult person in your organization, chances are they will disagree with your assessment, and see it as only your perspective. That's when you must present specific requirements and actions. You may not change their personality, but as the leader you have the right to expect certain healthy behaviors in your work environment.

Last, if the behavior doesn't change and you sense the impact on the organization is too great, release that person from their responsibility. If they are employed, carefully research and work through the termination process – legally and ethically. If the person is a volunteer then find the best way to gently and diplomatically end their participation on that team.

Take Away Realities

- Managing personnel requires constant nurturing.
- Assembling a team is a question of putting the right people in the right place.
- Review the qualities you're looking for in a team player, such as: Is this person teachable and does their persona reflect humility? Do they have a quality of character that reflects the organization? What relational skills and strengths do they bring to the table? Is creativity a desirable benefit for the particular job? Do they seem compatible with the current staff?
- Involve others in the decision making process to gain a broader perspective and insight.
- Defining expectations is the most basic component in the recipe for a healthy team.
- Motivation occurs when "it matters to them."
- *Dialogic follow up* means that we have a running conversation with our staff and continuously affirm or correct directions and trends.
- Constantly assess the impact of volunteers or employees and improve their capacity or release them from responsibility.

Core Questions for Personnel Management

1. If you're currently in a leadership role, list the things that have most surprised you about leading personnel. Have you served as an arbiter of interoffice problems? Were you successful or not, and what would you now do differently?

2. One of the core goals for leaders is to have everyone on board and moving in the same direction. Is this or can this be a reality in your organization? What has been the greatest deterrent to accomplishing this goal?

3. Consider your current team and give an honest assessment of how well you've assembled the players? (Use caution if this is discussed as a team.)

4. What qualities have you typically looked for in the hiring process? After reading this chapter, in what ways have you expanded your perspective?

5. Consider your review process of potential applicants, and describe what changes you might make.

6. As you evaluate your organization's culture and structure, do your employees and volunteers have a clear understanding of their roles, responsibilities, and expectations? What is lacking to better communicate the expectations?

7. What's the level of motivation in your organization? Are employees pulling their weight, giving more than expected, or is there a general malaise in the workplace? Project and describe potential strategies to increase the interest and commitment of your people.

8. Consider your method of performance review: has it been effective, successful, and led to performance changes? List several new options for evaluation and reflect upon which seems to fit you best. Would the dialogic method work for you? Why or why not?

9. If you have walked through the process of terminating someone, what have you learned as you reflect upon that experience? Did you wait too long, or move too quickly?

A Core Case for Mustering the Troops

Jack has struggled in his current leadership role. Though his previous stint as CEO of a large data systems company was very successful, profitable, and brought considerable recognition to him, his new job as the leader of a hunger relief organization wasn't going so well. He was unaccustomed to working with a sizeable volunteer roster, and the paid employees had all but crashed and burned in the interim before he arrived. The first month went well as he introduced himself and began to build working relationships with personnel. Months two and three were a blur with observation trips to third world countries. He, admittedly, felt the organizational day to day operations were slipping beyond his control. Now back in the office and well into the fourth month he's recognized there are some problems with key personnel. One who wanted the job he now held, and another who created considerable tension with a cynical attitude and a sharp tongue. Others were unsure of their roles in the organization and their future job security. Not only does Jack see more clearly the dysfunction, but he's finally willing to acknowledge that some of the personnel and volunteers are just not team players and have their own agendas.

      a. In your estimation, did Jack's schedule for the first few months lead to a healthy scenario for building a team?

      b. Based on the concepts of this chapter, how quickly should he deal with the office dysfunction? How could he begin to build his own team?

c. Describe a process that he could follow which would lead to regaining focus and direction for his team.

SECTION FOUR

Leading from Transparency

"Like a glass pane, transparency is the ability
to see through an outer layer in order
to view the inner workings of an organization
or the internal motives and actions of a leader."

CHAPTER 14

Transparency: The Glass House Effect

Though it's a metaphor, it's true: leaders live in glass houses, under the crucible of unrestricted scrutiny and are often subjected to different standards and expectations than the public. Christian leaders, in particular, have a unique set of principles based upon the morals of our scripture and the faith community to which we are accountable. The concept of "naked leadership" draws attention to the deeper parts of the leader's life that should be presented to the people in the organization.

In the political arena, we've seen heightened awareness and analysis of the private lives of candidates and current office holders. Some campaigns have derailed or busted because of revelations about the moral character of the leader. In Christian circles, recently, a number of ministries have come under suspicion or disrepute through revelations of dishonesty, moral failure, lavish living, or just plain old poor judgment. There has been a just call for

> *Christian leaders, in particular, have a unique set of principles based upon the morals of our scriptures and the faith community to which we are accountable.*

greater integrity among leaders, and this has certainly resulted in a need for transparency.

Like a glass pane, transparency is the ability to see through an outer layer in order to view the inner workings of an organization or the internal motives and actions of a leader. It is the opposite of opacity, which comes from purposefully hiding, blocking, or otherwise obscuring the machinations of your organization or your personal behavior. An opaque mentality shuts others out intentionally and cloaks motives by falsely displaying benevolent actions which are designed to mislead or manipulate.

The leader who desires transparency creates the opportunity for others to see behind the scenes and to look beyond the normal exterior of a ministry. It requires openness, vulnerability, congruency, integrity and accountability. There is a personal cost that goes with each of them.

The leader must first be open to transparency, and to be willing for one's life to be laid bare. Personal privacy is often forfeited or minimized. The leader still has a private life, but agrees to lower the barriers hiding him from those he serves. A move toward openness is an invitation for others to be a part of your inner world, and to join you in reaching the next level in your personal journey. It's also a significant way for the leader to begin building relationships with fellow travelers.

In religious life, the distinction between the laity and the clergy is an excellent learning point. For hundreds of years the clergy was more of a closed system of persons who were educated and trained to serve very specific roles in church life. In some denominational traditions, you couldn't be ordained unless you had the appropriate education. Occasionally, the religious vocations were filled with people who were not called by God, but who sought after a religious position as a "career." Nevertheless, the demarcating concept between clergy and laity developed, in which the ministers were clergy and the members were laity. The clergy were seen as "holy" because of their vocation. They were put on pedestals. They were often well educated and highly respected. Yet, the gap between the ordinary and divine widened as people didn't feel that they could live a "godly life" or do the work of the ministry. The differentiation between the sacred and secular became more pronounced and only the clergy could attain the status of sacred. As the "full time" clergy became the ministers of the mysterious gospel, market place ministry among the secular found little traction, because ordinary business men couldn't conceive of their vocation as a place for ministry.

Fortunately, a movement developed in which pastors desired to be understood, not as distinct or more holy, but as regular people called by God to do the Lord's work. The implications followed as ministers became more transparent: pastors and their families faced the normal struggles, disappointments, and same failures that others did. Confessional preaching from many pulpits invited people to learn from the pastor's struggles, to identify with the journey of their leader, and to join him in the pursuit of godliness, faithfulness and ministry to the world. Today, this openness has done much to encourage the laity that they, too, are ministers who are called to their "marketplace." They do not need a title, position, or education to be effective in reaching people.

This provides but one illustration as to the efficacy of openness. But let's be very real about transparency. It is a humbling place to be. It is also dangerous. It makes you vulnerable to those who could potentially exploit your "humanness" and self-professed weaknesses.

Transparent leadership, however, makes the most of this humanness. In fact, in some ways it releases the pressure to be perfect. Let's just admit this one up front: we're not perfect. Haven't been, won't ever be! It's a little freeing to accept that fact. I remember clearly a ministry oversight on my part: I missed a meeting where I was to open the building for an early morning group. It never hit my radar screen that morning. I apologized to the leader, whose response was comforting, "It's okay, it just let's us know you're human."

One of the chief goals of transparency is to let people know you, and they do want to know you. Your members or employees want to see who you are in the core of your being, and that you're human just like everyone else. In the organizational structure, and for a larger group of followers, there's an important relational transaction that takes place when people truly get to know the leader, not as a distant dictator but as someone who becomes flesh and blood to them. The incarnation model of Jesus as identified in the Gospel of John, chapter one, reminds us that God came to be with us. The text reads more literally, he pitched his tent among us. He became one of us, rubbed shoulders with us, felt our pain, and knew our destitution. He

> *Jesus - long before they understood his mission, they knew his heart.*

lived, worked, dwelt among those he desired to lead to a place of transformational change. The disciples grew to know him on an intimate level and long before they understood His mission, they knew His heart. They heard the angst in His voice when He chased the money changers from the temple. They felt His anguish at the death of Lazarus, and they saw the most succinct and revelatory moment of Jesus' time on the road with the disciples when he wept. They observed the determination that caused Him to set His face like flint toward Jerusalem. Jesus accomplished something special with the disciples, not unlike the relationships that are formed between the leaders and followers in your organization.

This relational transaction produces trust, empathy, loyalty, and investment. It leads to a two-way syncing of people's lives and purpose. After using a smart phone for many years, I'm well aware of the necessity of syncing my contact and calendar information with my phone and how that keeps me cross-checked on meetings and tasks. The leader, in building this kind of transparency, allows for the relational syncing that keeps everyone on the same page. Understand, also, that when the follower knows the leader on this deeper level, the leader's words take on new meaning. They are nuanced, filtered, and interpreted through the exposed heart, and through the follower's trust in the motives, intentions and perspectives of the leader. That knowledge of the leader's heart provides a subtext for the words, like a running commentary on everything the leader does and says.

That's why there must be a lack of deception and subversion on the leader's part. There is an integrated method of leadership transparency that helps overcome the pretext pitfalls or potential duplicity: a **congruency of your inner and outer world**. It's where you are the same person in both worlds. A requirement for this congruency is a careful examination of personal motives and ambitions and a consistent yielding and surrendering in humility to the Lord's direction. My will surrendered to His will, my thoughts surrendered to His thoughts, and my ambitions surrendered to His placement. It's where my personal agenda becomes displaced by His purpose.

Attitudes and behaviors begin to look the same whether one is alone in the prayer closet or standing in front of a group of board members. The treatment of others is respectful and consistent whether they are serving as a janitor or vice-president. We're the same in all worlds: inner and outer, public and private, home or work, secular or sacred. One of the most memorable compliments I've heard about myself came from my next door neighbor and good friend. It went something like this: Mark Gregory is the same when you see him at home as he is at work. Since my neighbor sees me mowing the yard and working on household projects, as well as being a member of the church I pastor, that's the kind of congruency I hope to foster.

Access is another essential element that naturally follows openness. Too often leaders become isolated from people in the organization. Whether it's a closed office door or a cloistered group insulating the leader, the perception is communicated clearly: you can't get to me,

I don't have time for you, or your input doesn't matter. All are damaging perceptions and cloud the transparency necessary for effective leadership. They also limit the ability to make wise and informed decisions, to know the pulse of the organization, and to react to appropriate needs of the followers.

The ancient Persian leaders devised a unique system whereby roads extending to the far reaches of the empire were prodigiously used by regional leaders known as "satrapies" who reported directly to the ruler. This road system and direct access from disparate parts of the empire provided a way for the king to make decisions with the best information and knowledge. From our perspective there's great benefit from frequently reaching beyond normal circles to get input that is independent and has an outsider's perspective. We shouldn't ignore our closest advisors, especially when they have proven their trustworthiness. Ensuring that we're not blind to a larger perspective is healthy.

I don't believe that "perception is reality," but I will concede that perception is an interpretive filter used by others to evaluate us. It influences us on many levels, including the emotional impact of other's decisions about us. As leaders, we must guard against the perception of aloofness, arrogance, or isolation. The way in which we allow people access to us is one determinate of that perception. Access is often restricted as the organization grows, and certainly the logistics of the larger churches or businesses make it more difficult for the leader to have

> *As leaders, we must guard against the perception of aloofness, arrogance, or isolation.*

time for every demand. But, there must be some mechanism whereby members can access the leader, or at the least where they're aware that it can be done. They know the process, and can be confident should a necessity arise, it's doable. Sometimes that alone is sufficient.

Consider the Roman Empire of the first century: the apostle Paul, as a Roman citizen, could appeal to Caesar and be granted an audience. This right resulted in a lengthy journey during which he effectively spread the gospel, and ultimately had his audience. I recently found myself on the other side of a leadership situation, in which I attempted to contact someone in a significantly larger organization. It was a difficult process that resulted in only partial success, and left me feeling disturbed about the lack of access to this leader. It reminded me of the need to develop an appropriate system that accomplishes and perpetuates availability to me by my congregation.

Furthermore, developing a means of consistent communication is helpful in reflecting a posture of transparency. Media-driven messaging is at our disposal today with: Twitter, Facebook, MySpace, Blogsites, websites, email and others. All give us a virtual interface with our members. A key is the consistency in which we dispense appropriate information. Creating and fulfilling an expectation of notifications puts people at ease, if they know they'll be kept informed and that the data is available if they are interested in accessing it.

I'm learning, also, there's a different perception dependant on whether you're in the loop or outside the loop. Our church leadership team meets regularly to discuss church matters, whether financial, personnel or strategic planning. Often we have general meetings without making any decisions or discovering any earth-shattering revelations. The assumption follows: there's nothing to report or communicate to the body.

From the "inside of the loop," it seems logical that no news is good news, or that if there's anything of significance that needs to be known, we'll pass it on. But I'm increasingly aware the perspective from "outside the loop" is like "what's going on around here?" To remedy that perception, I've made a personal commitment to begin blogging about church matters and attempt to disseminate information more fully. We've had a website since day one, and a Facebook account for several years, but we recently re-launched our website with a sharper look and consistently updated data. Our Facebook account has changed with almost daily postings of upcoming events, ministry signups, or deposits due; all in the attempt to get more info out the door and into the hands of our people. From a personal perspective, I've integrated my twitter, blog, and Facebook, and now feed my blog and twitter directly to my contact page on the church website. These are simple examples of how we can set up delivery systems for communicating with our people.

But is that enough? The method of delivery is important, but there must also be substantive content in the communiqué. Few things are more "off-putting" than attempting to answer a question and appearing to be evasive or holding back. It's probably better to admit up front that something is confidential or that you don't know the answer, rather than skirting the issue or speaking from ignorance. There's a delicate balance between sparse information that leads to suspicion and too much that drones on and dulls people's interest. Building trust and conveying the accuracy of your info is vital.

Communication is a four step process that I normally compact in the following way: *What you mean to say is not always what the other person thinks they heard you say.* The steps usually work in this manner: one person thinks, interprets, filters, and chooses words to say what they mean. The other hears the word choices, which in itself is then filtered, interpreted, and translated into meaning. Because of all the variables: word choices, tonal inflections, and body language, it's easy for the cycle to short circuit somewhere along the way. Great leaders and good communicators build relationships and create a connection with their audience. They find ways to speak their language and convey sincerity. If the leader is one who has a healthy track record with his audience, he is more likely to be received as authentic, and his words will bring satisfaction and understanding.

> *What you mean to say is not always what the other person thinks they heard you say.*

With the connection in place, effective leaders use strong content to back up their presentation. They bring reality into the equation, defining and clarifying the status of the organization; they hit head-on misconceptions and false assumptions. Positive trends and patterns of unhealthiness are willingly placed before people. Responsibility is accepted when necessary, and praise is given freely to others who have done their job well. The role of the leader is to bring light to darkness, and truthfulness to fabrication. If you want to be transparent, deception or subversion must be replaced by directness, accuracy, and reliability. Chasing rabbits or deflecting questions only lead to skepticism, which dims the glass of transparency rather quickly.

Transparency is easy to talk about, but harder to do. For it to be most effective, it takes time and persistent effort. Maintaining it is like standing on ice, it's slippery and melts from underneath you. So, put people in place around you who will help you build a transparent organization. Initiate the personal accountability that will help you keep it intact. Ask people you trust to give you a brutally honest assessment of how well it's going. Make it a priority!

Take Away Realities

- Christian leaders, in particular, have a unique set of principles based upon the morals of our scriptures and the community of faith to which we are accountable.
- Transparency is the ability to see through an outer layer in order to view the inner workings of an organization or the internal motives and actions of a leader.
- It requires openness, vulnerability, congruency, integrity and accountability; there's a personal cost that goes with each of them.
- One of the chief goals of transparency is to let people know you, and people truly want to know their leader.
- Work to attain a **congruency of your inner and outer world**. It's when you are the same person in both worlds.
- As leaders we must guard against the perception of aloofness, arrogance, or isolation.

Core Questions for Transparency

1. In your own words, write a definition for transparency. How does it match the concepts of this chapter? If not, explain why.
2. Should different vocations have distinct levels of morals, principles, and transparency?
3. Do you believe there is a personal cost to transparency? Give an example, either personal or hypothetical.
4. Reflect on the culture of corporate organizations, how accessible are the leaders? Does it benefit the culture of the group for the leader to be known by employees and volunteers?
5. On the following continuums place a mark that describes you. Write a short statement that reflects your answer.

Open	|------------------------|	Closed
Vulnerable	|------------------------|	Aloof
Present	|------------------------|	Distant
Accessible	|------------------------|	Isolated
Humble	|------------------------|	Arrogant

6. Conduct an honest assessment by asking: is there a congruency of your inner and outer world? Are you the same person in both? In what ways do people see you as the same or different?
7. Describe how communication can be an important part of transparency. Use words from the chapter such as content, truthfulness, connection, and rapport.

Mark W. Gregory

A Core Case For Transparency

The last leader of the group had failed miserably. He isolated himself from his employees and members, said and did things that he couldn't back up, and his personal integrity became questionable. The board has just elevated an associate into the executive position, and there was a sigh of relief from many of the workers. Jim had served in the organization for many years, was well respected, known for his truthfulness, and had already built solid relationships with other employees. He is preparing his first speech and is considering the things he should include. He wants to communicate vision and hope for the future, clarity of their present situation, and the necessary steps to get them back on track. But most importantly he wants to communicate something of who he is and how he will attempt to lead.

a. Place yourself in Jim's situation and write out (summarize) a first speech that sets the tone and communicates your hopes for the organization. What kinds of statements would you include that are self-revelatory and indicative of your own journey?

b. List strategies Jim could implement that promote transparency and create a new culture in that organization. For example, he could establish an open door policy for employees to have access to him.

CHAPTER 15

The Transparent Ingredient:
Trust at the Core

Among the many ingredients comprising transparency, trust is a building block of organizational health, while a lack of trust depletes the reserves quickly and fatally. When a new leader comes on board, there's a certain amount of trust inherit in the vetting process. Unless the leader has been forced on the organization, there's normally a carefully researched decision that leads to the appointment or election of the leader. Hopefully, the board, committee, or team who made the selection was held in high regard and procedurally walked the organization through a transparent process that fostered an initial trust of the new leader.

But the fundamental premises of trust are: it has to be both earned and maintained. Trust is a highly relational characteristic of the leader, and even in the best of situations, the new leader must prove himself as trustworthy. In church life, when a new pastor arrives on the scene, there's a shake-down period where the staff

> But the fundamental premises of trust are: it has to be both earned and maintained.

and members watch carefully the first actions and decisions of the leader. He is gauged by previous statements from the interview process, and how those

217

match his daily practice of leadership. It's an awkward dance, like two partners who stand at arm's length before familiarity leads to a fluidity of movement. Perceptions are formed and relationships are forged by the myriad of interactions. If those relational transactions are negative or forced, trust is diminished. If all goes well, the staff gives tacit trust to their new leader until it is somehow violated.

One of the first lessons I learned about trust relates to *consistency in personal actions*. As people observe my patterns or habits, they build a perception of how I will act in various situations based on my character and personality. If I then prove them correct over a period of time, I'm constructing a history they can rely upon. If my actions are "positively" consistent, this provides an expectation for future decisions, or more specifically, the way in which I will treat them as employees or members of my church. Truly, people catalogue and file away the things you do and how you respond to certain situations. This becomes the basis for their trust in you. Ultimately staff and members ask the question, "How will he treat me?"

This leads to a second aspect of consistency, *equity*, with the following question: "Will I be treated the same as everyone else?" (i.e. fairly, or equitably in comparison with other employees.) Few things start the downward spiral of trust than the perception of unfair or preferential treatment to some as compared to others. Regardless of reason or rationale, people take apparent slights very personally. Reversing the mistrust that develops is difficult, but if people know you treat others the same way, it diffuses the tension. By the way, this doesn't mean you are to treat everyone equally "bad." As followers of Christ, we are to show the grace and manner of our Lord in all our relationships.

The perception of inequity is why I tend to make decisions based on *principles* rather than *persons* - the *why* rather than *who*. A principles-based process guards against exceptions that may get you in trouble. Having asserted this, I do believe at times you default to the side of permission rather than prohibition. At Calvary, we often take the posture of allowing a person or ministry to take place until it creates an intervention moment, where we have to call it to a close. If you deviate from the normal expectations be prepared to explain why, or the confusion will erode the level of trust held in you.

From a communication standpoint, consistency is clearer when you *do what you say, and say what you do*. In previous chapters I discussed the verbal content of leadership, which includes a careful exposing of motives, and secondarily, ensures that you have something of worth to say that can be authenticated. It is obvious that to be caught in a lie is a major *faux pas*, but it's equally dangerous to be flippant with words by saying things you don't mean or by demeaning others to make yourself appear righteous.

People do not trust the leader they hear constantly complaining about others, because they wonder what the leader is saying about them in another context. Furthermore, if the leader makes claims that are not true, exaggerates circumstances for his own benefit, or doesn't follow through on promises, people are inclined to discount or outright disregard what he says. Words that are measured and meaningful add value to your leadership and build trust. The basics of building trust grows from healthy actions and decisions that build a history, carefully communicates the corporate reality and truth, and follows through on the assertions or promises made.

Once trust is lost, can it be reestablished? I have conducted a considerable amount of marriage counseling over the years, and I'm quick to affirm that trust can be rebuilt. But there are two caveats: it has to be earned, and it takes time. Here's the deal: if trust has been lost, it's usually because of a betrayal of relationship, disappointment due to destructive behaviors, or a misunderstanding resulting from poor communication. These three areas encompass a lot of territory, but the process of re-establishing trust is similar and overlaps thematically.

First you have to demonstrate that you're trustworthy, again. This starts with negotiating specific points to be upheld, whether words or behaviors. I usually begin with a list of items that prove the person's *transparency* and *accountability*. For example, one principle that I recommend to couples in counseling is the understanding that a spouse has an absolute right to know where the other person is at all times. For the person who hasn't lived under that restriction, it may seem unnecessary or invasive; however, in adulterous situations it's clearly a critical first step in establishing trust. In rebuilding the leadership trust level, the leader may voluntarily, or by negotiation with co-workers, make certain promises or set timelines to which he adheres, as a means of proving his trustworthiness. It may seem awkward to be accountable to a co-worker, but in essence you're just building a covenantal relationship with that person.

Time is not the great healer of all wounds, but real healing takes time. A proven record of new "rights" in contrast to old "wrongs" provides reassurance and releases anxiety as trust is built. I know of some people who quickly extend trust again to the offender, but most of us need a little time to process the hurt, come to terms with the deep wounds, and then slowly lower our guard again to reconnect. In my observation, there's an initial level of openness that people extend to those who are trying to rebuild trust, but it's usually tempered by a longer term suspicion or hesitancy. That's okay and normal. It may take months or even years for the restored trust to be fully in place.

> *Time is not the great healer of all wounds, but real healing takes time.*

Assuming that the leader has a second chance at building trust, accountability to an external group, council, or board is a good thing and restores confidence. We all benefit from knowing that our actions are under the scrutiny of someone else. It keeps us sharp; it makes us think another second before we jump headlong into a decision or situation; it's a preventative measure against our sometimes headstrong and destructive ways. When our people know that we have willingly submitted to that kind of authority, it's a re-affirmation of our sincerity, transparency, and trustworthiness.

Rebuilding trust certainly requires a change of the offending behavior. I often hear people say, "I'll believe it when I see it." I agree. It's a true statement. Behaviors must change. This is the angle of restoring trust where the leader begins a personal journey toward healing and healthiness. Leaders may have been involved in self-destructive actions or have struck out at others with verbal or even physical assaults. Intervention may lead to an abrupt halt of the offence, but long-term remapping of those behaviors is what really changes and strengthens the relational dynamic. If the behavior doesn't change, trust is not restored. This doesn't mean that the individual has to be perfect, and never make another mistake, but there must be an identifiable trend and discernable difference in attitude and behavior, and sometimes even in personality. If there has been an addictive facet of the behavior, then by all means, the addiction must cease and no longer hold influence in that person's life. Addiction, as a contributor to betrayal, is a pervasive and far-reaching culprit. While a termination of the abuse will bring some relief, the restoring of trust will take a longer and more persistent effort.

If the behavior is related to cynicism, bitterness, anger, or frustration resulting in caustic or harsh words between individuals, new patterns of speech will need to be developed. Some behaviors are deep seated and will require counseling to change harmful personality traits. Yet, we can learn to recognize when words hurt others and attempt to be encouraging rather than discouraging. It's troubling how harsh words can quickly wound, but the power of positive words is amazing.

The rebuilding of trust may be a simple as clarifying a misunderstanding between two people. Our personal sensitivities often prompt us to believe the worst of something that was said about us; we become offended, our hackles up, and flushed with anger. We would do well to work on our communication skills, the most important of which is to learn how to be a better listener. Then we can speak with a better perspective. In the height of verbal sparring, I often instruct couples to ask the question, "What's really going on here?" This simple question moves the conversation from the surface level angst to the deeper issues. It helps relieves pressure when the root of the conflict has been identified and can be addressed more specifically.

Restoring trust is a process, not an end point. It is an open-ended perpetual part of authentic relationships, and the person who considers it a part of the leadership journey has done well to include it. Trust is built layer upon layer, and there's really no end to the number of floors that can be constructed. In fact, the higher the building, the more likely the capability to weather minor disagreements or misunderstandings. It's worthy of our efforts to "earn" it and "maintain" it.

Take Away Realities

- Trust is a building block of organizational health, while a lack of trust depletes the reserves quickly and fatally.
- Trust has to be both earned and maintained.
- Trust relates to *consistency in personal actions*. As people observe patterns or habits, they build a perception of how we will act in various situations based on our character and personality.
- People construct a history of our actions and interpolate that to future decisions.
- Ultimately staff and members will ask the questions, "How will he treat me? Will I be treated the same as everyone else?" It's a matter of equity.
- In building trust, make decisions based on *principles* rather than *persons* - the *why* rather than *who*.
- Consistency is clearer when you *do what you say, and say what you do*. If the leader doesn't follow through on promises, people are inclined to discount or outright disregard what he says.
- To rebuild trust, you must demonstrate that you're trustworthy, again. This starts with negotiating specific points to be upheld, and behaviors to change.
- Time is not the great healer of all wounds, but real healing does take time.
- Accountability to an external group, council, or board is a good thing and restores confidence.

Core Questions for Trust

1. Describe a situation where you have seen trust displayed between the leader and members. What and who made that a healthy condition?

2. Consider the concept of *consistency in personal actions* as a component of trust building. In your personal history, what might you point to as evidence of your trustworthiness?

3. Reflect on a time when you were under someone else's leadership. Answer the questions: How was I treated? Was I treated equitably?

4. Describe a possible scenario where a decision is made by principles rather than on the basis of people – the why rather than who. Do you agree or not? Why?

5. Relate an experience where you saw the practice of this common statement: Do what you say, and say what you do. Relate an example where someone did not practice it.

6. Based on your actions and words, do your peers and followers discount or disregard the things you say?

7. If you've been in a situation where trust has been betrayed, what steps did you take that restored trust? List the concepts from this chapter and add to them from your own experience.

8. Being brutally honest and realistic, are you transparent and accountable?

9. Consider the statement that: restoring trust is not an end point, but a process. Do you agree? Why or why not?

Mark W. Gregory

A Core Case for Trust: The Transparent Ingredient

John Newby had led his non-profit organization faithfully for seven years. The society had grown tremendously with hundreds of new volunteers, and the staff looked to him to give guidance and direction. But he has been showing preferential treatment to a number of co-workers, letting some of their bad habits slide while at the same time adding pressure to other staffers to pick up the slack. He has begun raising his voice angrily with certain volunteers, expressing frustration at the lack of consistency in their schedules, and demanding that they either get on board or drop out of the group. A pattern of frustration and anger, which was not evident in the first six years of his leadership, had now stretched into six months of length.

The advisory board met with him and cautioned him about his outbursts and recommended that he receive counseling for anger management. After a month of counseling and no improvement, the board conducted a meeting and confronted him about his behavior. John broke down and admitted that he was dealing with an addiction to pain medication he received after a surgery the previous year. He had been desperately trying to deal with it on his own and was severely frustrated by his personal failure to conquer his abuse. The board now faced a dilemma concerning his continued employment and leadership.

> a. If you were an outside consultant, what steps
>   would you recommend the board take to

restore John to his position and rebuild trust in his leadership?

b. Assuming the board determined to continue John's employment, how might he rebuild relationships and trust among the co-workers and volunteers?

CHAPTER 16

———

nakedLEADERSHIP Reprised

We're back where we started. After fifteen chapters of personal soul-searching and an honest evaluation of our capabilities, we have not exhausted the scope of leadership, but we've certainly boarded the ship and set sail. You have been a part of my journey as I have written from my own experiences, and I hope that you have learned something new about yourself. In these last few pages, I want to reprise the main themes of this book as a way of re-focusing our attention on "naked leadership."

I'm most concerned about leaders who aren't yet sure of whom they really are at the core. I don't assume that you have "yourself" or "it" all figured out before you can be an effective leader. I do believe there are basic questions of personal identity that must be answered. The path that is the most authentically spiritual and sincere is rooted in the deepest relationship with Christ, and a uniqueness that is based on Him. For the person who is grounded there, leadership is filled with opportunities that God orchestrates, not what the leader forces or what men shape. The greatest danger is that we believe the worldly definitions that others impose upon us, rather than trust what God says about us.

The first chapters were challenging to me, in that now after thirty years of ministry and leadership, I'm laying out in print what really matters to me: the approval of God, not the approval of men. But, to keep that heartbeat is easier written about than executed. It helps when I trust Christ's perspective of my identity, and when I consider the re-definition of success.

Chapter one established that identity, and chapter two gave me a means to present it - in essence, to speak clearly of my heart and motives, to share the passions of my life in such a way that people (employees, volunteers, church members) know me, trust me, and are willing to walk with me. I know leadership really doesn't happen unless there is a journey, and from an organizational perspective, that people take the journey with me. So, the definition of leadership as presented in chapter three, prepares me for understanding the dynamic of chapter four: what is success? Here the contrast with the world's standard is clear. Success is not about an uptrend in raw numbers, or regal buildings overflowing with popular people, but is more about faithfulness to the call and claim that God has placed in our lives. For truly that is the standard of our judgment before the Lord. And to that I end, I desire to be true (I pray you will join me in that desire).

The second section of the book describes the process of initiating leadership, with a plunge into the hazard of forfeiting leadership followed by an explanation of leadership styles, skills, and traits. One huge misstep or a series of mishaps can disqualify us from leading. And painful are the ways we default by inaction and indecision. The best leadership is almost always proactive; yet when pushed to be reactive, we can do so based on the inherent character that we've cultivated in Christ. We know, too, our styles don't have the impact on us that we might have believed. We don't have to fit a certain mold to be successful, but it is important to understand whether we operate as demonstrative or communicative leaders, and how to adapt to the organizational growth needs. As described, the traits can be strengthened and developed. The good news is that we're not stuck as leaders! We can change, expand, learn, and even re-envision our futures.

Recently my wife, Jan, and I were talking about a friend and the stage of life that he's in concerning his leadership. Like me, he is beyond the "whippersnapper," "know-it-all" phase, and we are alike in our desire for ministry to linger long in our lives. At certain junctures you make honest evaluations of the leadership realities, and wonder, what should the next years of ministry look like? Jan's comment struck me as pertinent, not only for our friend, but for myself. "He should reinvent himself," she said. While we must always be true to who we are in Christ, she is absolutely correct in that leaders should always be learning, growing, changing, expanding, and reinventing themselves!

One of the ways to manage that process of reinvention is by periodically reviewing the core identity issues from the first section, and by sharpening some of our essential leadership traits: passion, humility, creativity and intuition. Passion can diminish, and like an ember when removed from the fire and turns to blackened wood, it can die. But new passions can emerge and old ones can be relit. Humility is an intensely personal spiritual concern that comes from surrender. Creativity, which stands on the three pillars can flourish as the leader creates space to allow it. And intuition can be developed as we learn to trust what our senses are telling us.

All of this comes to fruition as we are planted in a particular leadership soil - often ground that has lain fallow for some length of time, or that has grown contaminated by the pollution of the last leader's oil spill. When we built our first phase facility at Calvary, one of the important considerations was an environmental study: were there any old fuel tanks or oil dumps on the land; was there anything toxic such as pesticides that remained from earlier farming operations? Likewise in every new organizational pursuit: what's the lay of the land, where are the toxic spills, traps, snares and deadfalls? It takes an in-depth look at the environment and culture of your group, followed by an assessment of the challenges and changes that must be navigated. It sometimes takes a brave, adventuresome, and battle-seasoned captain to remain at the helm until the ship reaches port. As captain, the building of a team is critical to the process of transition and change. Make every effort to hire the right people based on the criteria that are presented in chapter thirteen.

As a return to the realities of leadership, if you're going to accomplish anything it will happen because you've built trust for the journey by being transparent with your people. Remember one thought from an earlier chapter – committed followers are those who "know the vision, *trust the leader*, and whose personal spiritual journey aligns with the long-term goal of the organization." Transparency and trust are essential ingredients in the process, and the strongest predictors of confidence in the leader are the measures of accessibility, vulnerability, and transparency presented by the leader.

This book has helped me solidify my thoughts on leadership, and forced me to rethink some of my own habits and patterns. It's been a healthy process of self-examination and self-disclosure. I don't presume to understand myself fully, but I've sure gained some ground and rounded out some of my individual rough spots. That's what we as leaders must do: keep moving forward personally. How can we expect our organizations to grow if we're not! That's my determination. What about you?

If you're on a leadership journey, consider for yourself the voyage past, present and future. Are you stuck in a sheltered bay while the hurricane blows by, or are you moving under the full furl of the windblown sail. Have the seas been calm and you're drifting, waiting for some fortunate wind to change? As I think about you, the reader of this book, the picture I have is of myself standing on the dock watching the ships maneuver into port. I hope to see you standing at the helm – and we'll declare you the leader!

Author's Note

No book is written in isolation, and that is certainly true with nakedLEADERSHIP. I appreciate the many reviewers who provided critical feedback, guidance and most of all, encouragement. They will find that a number of their suggestions were incorporated into the project. I also want to thank Connie Wright and Dianne Lamb who poured over the manuscript with a critical editing eye. Their notations were carefully evaluated and utilized. Thanks to you all!

The idea for the book originated when I was invited to be a guest lecturer in leadership classes taught at Middle Tennessee State University by Dr. Watson Harris. The students were required to submit, in advance, questions they wanted me to address. I noted the similar nature of the submittals from each of the sessions and concluded that most students of leadership have the same basic questions. I began compiling my answers in notebook form for the presentations. The process of writing nakedLEADERSHIP started as I desired to impart to my sons the concepts that I had been formulating. I hope that one day they will pull this book from the shelf to glean what their dad had to say about leadership. For this reason, this book is dedicated to my sons, Daniel and Scott.

August, 2010